VISION AND CHARACTER

VISION AND CHARACTER:
A CHRISTIAN EDUCATOR'S
ALTERNATIVE TO KOHLBERG

Craig R. Dykstra

PAULIST PRESS
New York/Ramsey

The Publisher gratefully acknowledges the use of the following materials:

Excerpt from an address by Dr. Edward A. Robinson, "The Poet and the Policeman," Wrexham, England, April, 1974. Used by permission.

Excerpt from *Toward Moral and Religious Maturity* by Stanley Hauerwas, *et al.*, copyright © 1980 Silver Burdett Company. Used by permission.

Part of the first chapter originally appeared in "Moral Virtue or Social Reasoning" in *Religious Education* 75 (March–April 1980):2. Used by permission.

Library of Congress
Catalog Card Number: 81-82340

ISBN: 0-8091-2405-X

Published by Paulist Press
545 Island Road, Ramsey, N.J. 07446

Printed and bound in the
United States of America

Contents

Acknowledgements

This book is a thorough revision of a dissertation that I presented to the faculty of Princeton Theological Seminary in 1978. Although much of the present work does not appear in the former, neither could have been done without the guidance, criticism, and support of my teachers at Princeton. I want to express my grateful appreciation, therefore, to Professors D. Campbell Wyckoff, Diogenes Allen, and James E. Loder. The personal and professional support and encouragement given me in innumerable ways by Dr. Wyckoff, in particular, has been greater than anyone could expect.

Part of the first chapter of this book was previously published as "Moral Virtue or Social Reasoning" in *Religious Education* 75 (March–April 1980): 2. I am grateful to the Religious Education Association for permission to use this material again here.

I have been privileged for the past three years to be a member of the Faculty of Louisville Presbyterian Theological Seminary. The seminary has afforded me time to work by granting a sabbatical leave. It has helped me in preparing the manuscript for publication by providing funds and assistance for typing and duplication. But more than any of this, the seminary is a place where one can work with students and colleagues in an atmosphere of friendship, mutual concern, and healthy stimulation. For all of this, I am sincerely grateful. Special thanks are due to President C. Ellis Nelson, who read the dissertation and assisted me in publishing; to Dr. Louis Weeks and Ernest White, who read and provided valuable criticism of the manuscript; and to Brenda Alexander and Marti Marsh, who took on the chore of typing.

For my family, I reserve my deepest gratitude. My parents have provided moral, spiritual, and material help for many years; and it would be impossible for me to express my thankfulness for them adequately. My sons, Peter and Andrew, have more than once come down to my study to ask me why I had to write this book, implying that I would be much better off if we all played catch. When I took their advice, I found it easier to write when I returned. I am grateful for their assistance. My wife, Betsy, is my life partner. In this venture of writing she has given much more than she has received. With patience, encouragement, grace, and good cheer she has, amidst her many other responsibilities, upheld me. For these people especially, I thank God; and to them I dedicate this book.

Craig R. Dykstra
Louisville, Kentucky
October, 1980

Introduction

When some ethicists survey the moral terrain, they get their bearings and set out their markers by using such concepts as principles, rights and duties, justice and injustice, conflicts and claims, decisions, judgments, reasons and justifications, roles and acts. When another group of moral philosophers look out over the moral life, they see it rather differently, and use a different language to describe it and to find their way in it. They use words like convictions and meanings, responsibility, good and evil, contexts, vision, stories and images, character, virtue, and ways of being.

The two groups are not looking in different directions or living on different planets. The differences rather resemble those between two artists who paint the same landscape, but do so quite differently because they focus on different dimensions of it and see in it different patterns of texture, color, and coherence. Because they focus and perceive differently, they represent the landscape differently in their paintings. And in order to do that, they need to use different artistic techniques and materials. Something similar, I think, goes on in moral philosophy.

There is no one widely used name for each of these two styles of doing moral philosophy. The first often goes under the name of deontological ethics; but it is also characterized as "formalistic ethics" or as an "ethic of decision-making," depending on which aspect of it a particular philosopher or critic wishes to highlight. The second has also assumed a variety of aliases: "character ethics," "responsibility ethics," and "ethic of virtue," to name a few. The names are not as important as the idea that there are two, fundamentally contrasting ways of seeing the moral life and of doing moral philosophy. I shall give them the names *juridical ethics and visional ethics* as a shorthand.[1] These names point to what I think is the

1

decisive difference between the two. In juridical ethics, the focus is on making judgments about the rightness or wrongness of particular acts as a judge in a law court might do. The focus in visional ethics is on the way one sees reality and responds to it in the light of that vision.

Whether one approaches the moral life from the point of view of juridical ethics or that of visional ethics makes a very great difference in how one understands moral development and moral education. Recent work in these areas has been almost completely dominated by the point of view of juridical ethics. The work of the Harvard social psychologist Lawrence Kohlberg is the prime example. The moral life is, for him, primarily the life of making choices about how to act in situations where people's claims about rights and duties conflict. Moral development is the development of the ability to provide increasingly more principled reasons and justifications for the choices one makes in such situations. His work from this perspective has stimulated vital new interest in moral psychology and moral education. A vast literature has grown up around it, and new educational efforts are now being made in schools and other social institutions on the basis of the theories that he has worked out.

Kohlberg's approach has likewise had an impact on religious education. Articles and books describing the value of this point of view for understanding moral education in the context of religious communities have proliferated. They range from scholarly analyses to popular attempts to inform the ordinary church-school teacher of its implications for the classroom. Curriculum designs in religious education also call attention to the need to construct educational experiences in terms of the Kohlberg thesis.

Kohlberg's influence on religious educators is in some ways a bit surprising. Religious people have generally assumed some intimate connection between the religious and the moral in their lives. They have felt that their religion has something to do with the kind of people they are and the way they live their lives, including the way in which they live in relation to other people. Since the Enlightenment, however, there has been a steady attack on the assumption that the religious life and the moral life are intimately connected. This attack has come in large part from the juridical tradition in ethics. In Kohlberg's work, the philosophical side of this attack converges with a rationalistic strain in developmental psychology.[2] The result is a theory of moral development that finds little room for any substantial religious connection at all, and ends up being limited as a foundation for Christian education for the moral life.

The juridical tradition in ethics, including Kohlberg's version of it, is a respectable position. But it is not the only one. My purpose in this book is to carry out a line of exploration that examines the alternative perspective. What might moral education and moral growth look like if we used visional ethics as our guideline rather than juridical ethics? I approach this task primarily as a Christian educator. This means that my conviction about which kind of ethics is most adequate is not disinterested. I want to know how the resources of the Christian faith and community can most powerfully and fruitfully be brought to bear in education for the moral life. I believe that visional ethics helps us to make constructive sense of our intuition that the religious and the moral are intimately connected. It can also help us to see why and how worship and prayer, confession and repentance, biblical and theological study and interpretation, fellowship and discipleship, are important for moral growth and in moral education. But I do not advocate visional ethics primarily for utilitarian reasons. I am convinced that visional ethics provides a richer, more adequate representation of what the moral life is like for us. By focusing differently, it accounts for more of what the moral life involves and more truly describes how we struggle as moral human beings.

In order to set the stage for the work on the relation between visional ethics and moral growth and education, it will be helpful first to survey some of the basic assumptions of the juridical approach in Kohlberg's theory of moral development.[3] In this context, I will have some criticisms to make. This task will comprise Part I.

In Part II, I will present a theological understanding of the moral life based in the ethics of vision. Some of its major themes will be charted. Some of its implications for moral growth and moral transformation will be developed. Because the moral domain is much more broadly understood in visional ethics than in juridical ethics, no one psychological school corresponds neatly with it. This makes the task of a moral psychology of visional ethics extremely difficult, and one that cannot be undertaken with any degree of completeness here. We will have to be satisfied at this point with fits and starts, hunches and leads. Anything like the elegance of Kohlberg's stage theory is impossible in such an exploration. I once thought this to be a weakness. I have discovered, however, that the elegance of Kohlberg's approach is gained partially at the expense of a rich description of the manifold complexities of the moral life as we actually experience it.

Part III moves toward a theory of Christian education for the moral life, and concludes with some suggestions for the practice of moral education in the Christian community.

This book is written primarily for religious educators, especially Christian religious educators. My ultimate target is education for the moral life in the Christian community. The fact that I write for religious educators and from the point of view of Christian faith does not mean, however, that I believe only Christians can be moral or that a Christian ethic is the only sound ethic. I want to suggest that our ethics, and therefore our understanding of moral development and our way of doing moral education, properly grows out of the vision of reality that a particular community holds. If this perspective seems justified from the argument of the book, then educators from other communities may be interested not only in my critique of Kohlberg, but also in visional ethics as a paradigm for moral development and education.

Because the book is written for religious educators, it will not read like one written for moral philosophers, religious ethicists, or developmental psychologists. There are many technical philosophical, theological, and psychological issues involved in this discussion, and it is impossible to avoid them. But I have tried to put these issues in accessible language, and have used the end notes to refer to sources for those who wish to deal with them more technically.

I   CRITICISM

1
Kohlberg's Juridical Ethics: A Critique

Every conception of the moral life presupposes some understanding of what the central features of morality are and of what the nature of a moral person is. Lawrence Kohlberg's theories of moral development and moral education are no exception. His theories contain explicit definitions of what it means to be moral, what it means to be morally mature, and what it takes by way of experience and development to become so.

Kohlberg's juridical ethics achieves clarity on these issues by raising to marked prominence the dilemmas, decisions, choices or problems people encounter in social relationships, and by focusing almost entirely on situations in which those occur. Because of this, the moral landscape is seen to consist largely of problematic circumstances. Morality becomes the enterprise of social problem solving, and ethics becomes the discipline of finding the most adequate ways to solve those problems. Juridical ethics asks such questions as: What is the problem here? What are alternative ways of dealing with it? Which one should be chosen? On what grounds? Are those grounds adequate? Problems plead for solutions. Juridical ethics is mainly interested in how we can best find them.

A concept of the moral person goes along with this. The moral self for juridical ethics is a problem-solving agent, a kind of judge who is able to weigh in the balance the various aspects of a problem and make a decision about what ought to be done to solve it most fairly. Such an image of the moral person carries with it some implications concerning what capacities and characteristics are to be valued most highly in people. To be a good judge one must be skilled in seeing all the sides of an issue, in deciding which interests are most important, and in providing reasons for the decisions that other people can understand and examine for themselves. Because good judges are like this, juridical ethics places a premium on human capacities for analytical reasoning, disinterested judgment, decisiveness of will, and rational discourse.

Although Kohlberg is quite clear about what he thinks morality is and what it takes to be a moral person, he does not seem to have recognized that his picture of the moral landscape and his image of the moral person are a function of the general moral vision of juridical ethics rather than a simple description of morality just as everybody sees it. Not everyone does have this picture of the moral life, and the alternative pictures are not less well founded. This chapter examines critically some basic claims that Kohlberg makes as well as the general picture of the moral life that lies behind those claims. At the core of Kohlberg's theory of moral development lie three key claims that are mutually confirming. If they are accepted, it becomes difficult to dispute Kohlberg's general conception of the nature of moral development. If these claims can be refuted, however, the way opens for an alternative conception of moral development.

The first claim is *philosophical* in nature and has to do with the definition of morality. For Kohlberg, virtue, or moral goodness, is ultimately one thing, namely, knowledge of the ideal of justice defined as the right of every person to equal consideration of his or her claims in every situation.[1] The second claim is *psychological,* and runs as follows: There is one psychological structure of morality, which is defined as the cognitive pattern of organization for processing information or for connecting experienced events in terms of equality or reciprocity between selves with expectations of one another.[2] If we want to know about the psychology of morality, this pattern of cognitive organization (or structure) is what we ought to study. The third claim is *operational:* The best and only adequate way to study these structures (and, hence, moral development) is to observe and analyze people's verbally expressed judgments about situations in which people have claims on one another.[3]

The mutually confirming nature of these three claims is note-worthy. Virtue is one, and the psychological structure of morality is unitary. Virtue is knowledge, the psychological structure of morality is cognitive, and the testing technique involves eliciting and analyz-ing people's cognitive judgments and patterns of reasoning. The content of the knowledge that is virtue is justice defined in terms of equality or reciprocity of rights; that which is cognitively organized in the psychological structure is information and events in terms of equality or fairness in situations where people have expectations of others (that is, where they claim rights); and the dilemmas that elicit the judgments studied are dilemmas involving conflicting claims or rights. This congruence is the reason Kohlberg feels justified in arguing that there is a parallelism between his theory of psychologi-cal development and his moral philosophy,[4] and that what he is studying when he studies people's responses to the moral dilemmas he gives them is their moral development. The parallelism is there from the beginning—by definition.

Since the three claims are mutually confirming, it becomes clear that, if all three are true, Kohlberg has a highly consistent and convincing point of view. But if any one of these claims can be shown to be inadequate, the internal structure of the theory begins to collapse. For example, if virtue is not ultimately one thing (the ideal of justice defined in terms of equal rights), but rather a number of things defined in a variety of ways, then a study of the cognitive structures used for processing information about rights and duties will give us, at best, only a partial understanding of moral develop-ment. I wish to argue that, indeed, the internal structure of Kohl-berg's theory does collapse because all three of his fundamental claims are false.

The Philosophical Claim

Kohlberg claims that virtue is one thing, namely, knowledge of the ideal of justice. Is this so? It seems odd, at least. Philosophers and lay persons alike have always been able to list a variety of virtues that seem to be distinct but that all seem necessary for what we mean by morally good or morally mature people. William Alston says, in his "Comments on Kohlberg," that

> it is notorious that moral philosophers agree no more about what is distinctive of the moral than about anything else; and a large number of distinct accounts of what makes a judgment, a reason, an attitude, a rule, or a principle moral have been put forward. Kohlberg chooses one of these . . . but fails to do anything by way of showing that this is more than a choice of what seems most congenial or interesting to him.[5]

Kohlberg enlists, in his defense, Socrates and Plato as adherents of his view that virtue is one.[6] But a close look shows that Kohlberg does not express a Platonic view. Plato, unlike Kohlberg, accepts a variety of virtues and is willing to name them: wisdom, temperance, courage, justice, and piety.[7] Plato is concerned with the unity of the virtues, but Kohlberg misinterprets what Plato means by this. Plato wants to know what makes all of these elements virtues. Kohlberg's answer is that they all are synonyms for the same thing, knowing justice. But this is not Plato's answer.

For all of Plato's concern with justice, justice does not, for him, stand alone. Justice stands with the other virtues or it does not stand at all. Justice without wisdom, temperance, courage, and piety is not possible. A person cannot be both cowardly and just, for example. But the fact that justice, wisdom, temperance, courage, and piety always stand together does not mean that they are identical. Their unity does not mean that they can all, in the end, be reduced to one thing. Rather, their unity consists of the fact that they are all present simultaneously in the good person. The virtuous person has all of them, or none. Thus, the unity of the virtues in Plato is a reference to the unity of character in the good person, so that whoever is wise, temperate, courageous, pious, and just is virtuous or good. Only the person who possesses all of these qualities is truly good or morally mature.[8]

Plato is right at this juncture, and Kohlberg is wrong. Morality is something we ascribe to people, and people are more than what they know. What they know and how they use what they know is conditioned by who they are. And who they are depends on the way in which a number of distinct qualities come together in them. Kenneth Keniston reminds us of people

> whom we know from personal experience or from history who seem truly post-conventional in moral reasoning, but whose genuine adherence to the highest moral values is not matched by compassion, sympathy, capacity for love and empathy. In such individuals, the danger of breaking human eggs to make a moral omelet, of injuring people in order to advance one's own moral principles, is all too real.[9]

Virtue is not just the knowledge of the ideal of justice. We need not only to know what is just. We also need to care for justice with such depth that our lives can be lived justly even when it costs us dearly—and that takes courage. Furthermore, the justice that we live must be a justice that is attentive to the real needs of the people with whom we live—and that takes qualities of wisdom and compassion, which the capacity to adjudicate the claims of parties in a situation does not automatically entail. Finally, justice also requires a kind of piety—a sense that there is an order to the world that must be respected, a sense of gratitude for the givenness of it, and a sense of wonder toward and honor to the Giver. In sum, virtue may be one, but justice is not its only name.[10]

In addition to the inadequacy of Kohlberg's claim that virtue can be defined solely as the knowledge of justice, there is something else wrong with his philosophical claim. His understanding of what justice is, is far too limited. Partly, this is a result of his approach to moral language.

There are two basic—and fundamentally different—ways of understanding the relationship between words and what those words mean: the *conventional* and the *symbolic.* The conventional approach suggests that words are given meaning by common consent. We decide what words mean by public agreement. If we want to know what a word means, we look at the way that word is ordinarily used in public discourse, analyze the public rules and reasons for its appropriate use, and follow them when we use the word. The symbolic approach is quite different. This approach argues that we use words (some words, at least) to refer to realities that transcend us and that we cannot fully apprehend or comprehend. We do not necessarily agree on what words mean. They may take on different meanings in different contexts and perhaps new and deeper meanings in the light of experiences that others may not have had. In this case, words do not simply put a name on what everyone already knows. They point toward realities that must be experienced in depth if the words are to be understood. Here words do not exhaust meaning; they open us up to meaning.

Take the word *justice.* Kohlberg defines it conventionally. For him, justice is the equal consideration of every person's claims in a situation where people's claims conflict. Justice is "a universal mode of choosing, a rule of choosing which we want all people to adopt in all situations."[11] Kohlberg can state specifically what it takes to follow that rule.[12] The meaning of the word is exhausted by the definition, and the word points to no deeper reality than the public rule for its appropriate use. Anyone who can understand the rule knows what it means to be just.

The effect of this approach to definition is seriously reductive. It defines the concept in terms of what rational people, just by virtue of their being rational, can understand it to mean. This approach does not regard any particular personal and, perhaps, private experience that persons may have had. But might it not be true that having certain kinds of experiences puts us into a position to know the meaning of justice more deeply and, in fact, in a way that is different from other people's knowledge of it? Might not justice be a reality of great depth that transcends us and that we cannot fully comprehend? The witness of the heritage of Jewish and Christian faith claims that it is.

Only after Job endured extreme hardship and affliction could he apprehend a justice of God that he could not, when he was prosperous, even suspect. Even at the end of the book, Job could not articulate what he had seen (Job 40:3). But he realized that he had been confronted by a reality of justice greater than anything he had ever known:

> I talked about great things I did not understand, about marvels too great for me to know. You told me to listen while you spoke and to try to answer your questions. Then I only knew what others had told me, but now I have seen you with my own eyes. (Job 42:3b–5)

The same may be true for us. It may be only when we have suffered, sacrificed, been afflicted, or been faced with imminent death that we have any idea what justice at its deepest is. We do not know simply by knowing the meaning of the rule. The knowledge of justice, which is more than a knowledge of how fairly to adjudicate the claims of competing parties, presupposes experiences that we have only through great discipline and great risk. It may also presuppose a certain relationship to God and to the world.

The Bible has no conception of justice apart from a covenantal relationship that undergirds it. Justice is conditioned and shaped by the covenantal relationship that the people have with God. This conditioning and shaping cuts two ways. First, human beings cannot understand what justice means unless the meaning of God's justice is first revealed. But God's justice is not always easy to discern. As both Abraham and Job found out, God's justice sometimes "goes deeper than man is able to penetrate."[13] Second, God's justice cannot be revealed unless persons are themselves restored by God to the covenantal relationship with God. Restoration is the effect of God's justice, or righteousness. Thus, human justice depends on divine justice for both its meaning and its possibility. Justice can neither be known nor done simply by knowing the rule. It depends on both God's action and a responding transformation of our whole selves in relation to God.

It is not possible here to spell out the whole of the Old and New Testament understandings of justice. But a deep tradition in our own religious understanding maintains that the transcendent reality of God's justice is both an inexhaustible mystery and the lodestar by which our own moral lives are guided and toward which our concepts for articulating it point. A conventional definition of justice simply cannot reveal these dimensions.

Kohlberg, of course, recognizes that concepts like justice have increasingly deeper and more complex meanings. His whole stage theory is an argument that development involves the increasing capacity to plumb those depths. My disagreement with Kohlberg concerns his claim to have exhausted those depths with his most developed (i.e., Stage 6) understanding of justice. Justice means much more than the correlation of rights and duties when the concept is set in the context of an ongoing covenant with a God who transcends us and to whom we need to be rightly related.

Another reason why Kohlberg's understanding of justice is inadequate is also connected to the conventional approach to definition, but in a different way. A definition of justice that depends on public rules and reasons for its application requires that the claims being disputed must be articulated in such a way that any objective, rational moral agent could understand their meaning, no matter how he or she is related to the person making the claims. The problem with this requirement is that there are moral cases in which the claims are not clear and cannot be made clear in a publicly articulable manner without reducing those claims to something else.

Consider the following case. A wife feels she is being used. After a long period of wondering what she has done wrong and whether it is her fault, she cries out to her husband: "You pay no attention to me. You act as if I am not really here. I feel that I am just an object to you, something useful to have around." But he does not understand, or perhaps simply pretends not to understand: "What do you want from me? I have given you everything. Time, a house, children, money—everything I have is yours! What else do you want?" If you know of circumstances like these, you know that the wife cannot respond with any list of things for him to give her, or actions for him to perform. No such series, even if it were infinite, would give her what she needs. In frustration, she blurts out, "What I want, what I need, is you!" She needs his presence—his love, if you will. She needs him in such a way that he does not make her feel like a stranger or an object to him, or him to her.

So long as justice is understood to involve only the meeting of the objective and publicly articulable needs of persons with objectively definable acts and goods, then the Kohlbergian understanding of justice is adequate.But as soon as we enter the realm of intersubjective relationships where it matters who in particular is making the claim, who in particular the claim is being made of, and where the need cannot be met by providing objectively definable acts and goods, then a conventional, public, objective, universalizable conception of justice becomes inadequate.

The fact of the matter is that a very great portion of the situations that make up our moral lives are of the intersubjective rather than the objective kind. They are all the situations we live in, in which it matters that particular people are involved rather than anonymous actors who play roles in a drama that has no past and no future beyond the immediate problem. How we live with our spouses, our children, our colleagues, and friends in everyday living has a great deal to do with who we are as moral beings. Indeed, what we do and how we think and feel in this intersubjective realm may go very far in determining how we will react when more public moral crises and dilemmas face us.

The Psychological Claim

Kohlberg's psychological claim is that there is one psychological structure of morality. That is defined as the cognitive pattern of organization each of us has for processing information or for connecting experienced events in terms of equality or reciprocity between selves with expectations of one another. A corollary to this claim, one for which Kohlberg also argues, is that the level of transformation (the stage) one has achieved in the development of this structure is the determinant of one's moral maturity.

If what I have said about Kohlberg's philosophical claim is true, if virtue is not one thing in the sense Kohlberg means it, then one must conclude that Kohlberg's claim to have isolated the core psychological structure of morality must be false as well. The capacity cognitively to organize information and connect events in terms of reciprocity at its most complex level is not a *sufficient* condition for moral maturity. But even if this point is accepted, one might still argue that the development of this structure is a *necessary* condition for moral maturity, in fact, the most critical necessary condition. It is as if someone might say,"All right, that may not be all there is to moral maturity. But what Kohlberg has identified has certainly got to be part of it, and maybe the most important part." I want to propose that it is not even a necessary condition. People can be morally mature, exemplars of moral goodness, without having the capacity to organize information and events in the way Kohlberg says they must at the highest stages.

It is important to be clear on this issue if we are to have a sufficiently rich and comprehensive theory of moral development. Iris Murdoch once said that "if moral philosophy does not give a satisfactory account of what we unphilosophically know to be goodness, then away with it."[14] The same holds true for theories of moral development. We should not let the theory define for us what moral goodness is, and then evaluate a person's moral maturity on that basis. We should require of a theory that it adequately reflect what we untheoretically know to be goodness. It seems to me that there are people whom we know to be morally insightful and courageous who do not fit well into the upper strata of the Kohlberg schema. I am thinking, for example, of some poorly educated, analytically unsophisticated people whose actions exhibit a kind of deep compassion and rare advocacy for human welfare in circumstances of considerable personal risk that most of us who reason and talk well are never up to.[15]

The key to Kohlberg's conception of the psychological core of moral judgment is the understanding of objectivity that he borrows from Jean Piaget, the Swiss developmental psychologist. Objectivity, by this account, depends on cognitive reversibility. Reversibility in cognitive operations means the ability to "move back and forth between premises and conclusions without distortion."[16] In moral thought, Kohlberg claims, reversibility is this same ability with reference to the various claims people make in a situation of social conflict. It is the ability to move among all of the various points of view in a conflictual situation, imaginatively putting everyone in everyone else's shoes, and correlating everyone's rights with everyone's duties.

But there are two prerequisites for reversible thought in any domain: It must be conscious, and it must concern itself with objects of publicly identifiable and articulable claims. Hence, reversible thinking as the paradigm of knowing presupposes a particular vision of what is real.

> Reversibility is . . . a concept of objectivity which naturally goes with a picture of the real as a system which can undergo a coherent set of transformations. . . . And to see the world objectively is to see it as . . . something which would ideally be manipulable in a coherent way.[17]

This expectation of manipulability is precisely what makes it impossible for the higher-stage cognitive processes to deal adequately with such intersubjective moral situations as the case between the husband and the wife. In order to deal with the wife's claims objectively, the husband must, in effect, say: "Make yourself into an object so that I may know what specifiable actions I need to undertake in order to treat you justly." Kohlberg's notion of the ideal psychological end point of moral development requires that persons become objects in order for moral decision and action to take place. This, of course, is just what the wife resists as a form of immoral treatment.[18]

A good number of the situations in which we have to make moral decisions can, of course, be understood objectively in this sense without distortion. In these cases, the capacity for reversible thought can be very helpful in making those decisions. But, insofar as reversible thought leads us to expect that all moral situations are objectively manipulable, it may actually be a very great hindrance to moral insight and action. Bill Puka describes one aspect of this:

> From the moral point of view in role-taking we must not only be able to recognize that others have a point of view, or even what that point of view is, but to assume that point of view fully. We must regard that person's welfare from their point of view with a degree of self-interest not uncomparable to that we display for ourselves from our point of view. This is what it is to respect persons, to take them seriously. It is incredibly easy not to do this and to believe wholeheartedly that one has. . . . What higher stages pro-

vide the rationalizer . . . is an invulnerable refuge for self-deception as well as the deception and misleading of others.[19]

The deception comes through the insistence that all reality is a coherent set of manipulable transformations when, in fact, it is not.

If reversible cognitive processes are not the key to moral maturity, what is? Here we have to be very cautious. First, if a plurality of virtues comes together in particular people to make them virtuous, we should expect that virtuous people have a number of important psychological characteristics that are all relevant to their virtue. There may also be certain kinds of concrete experiences that enhance those capacities and provide occasions for their actualization. Second, we need to pay heed to Robert Cole's important warning. With reference to a "thoroughly uneducated Negro sharecropper" who took singular risks "in the face of his state's segregationist 'justice,' " Coles says:

> To examine his "morality" would require so subtle a knowledge of his thought and action that I really think the deliberate vagueness of the word "spirit" or "character" to be more accurate: he had spirit in him, he was a man of character. The details of his childhood, the facts of his social and economic existence, the cultural ambience he shares with his family and friends . . . all of those "factors" simply fail to ignite that one man, his morality, actively expressed, timidly justified, poorly explained.
>
> I think that is one of the chief troubles we have these days; the sources of dignity and ethical responsibility are not really known, despite all our interest in the mind.[20]

> What makes for merciful people and for courageous people is for me very much a mystery, in spite of all we know (and claim to know) about the inside of man's body and mind and the outside of the world he inhabits.[21]

Nonetheless, it is important to play some hunches if we play them with humility. More will be said about this later, but I suspect that the key in terms of cognitive operations is not formal, reversible thought, but the capacity for imaginal thought. This takes various forms in adult life, but first becomes available at around the age of three with the emergence of what Piaget calls the "symbolic function." Charles Taylor argues that imaginal thought helps us to deal with a moral situation, not by objectifying it, but by helping us "come to see and feel it in a different way, or ... to see it as something different, and hence to live it in a different way."[22]

By virtue of imaginal thought, we come to see things from a different perspective, and perhaps to see into things more deeply. In situations where we are significantly self-involved, this may be the only way to see, interpret, understand, choose, and act realistically. The nature of many moral situations is such that

> we cannot abstract from their significance to us without shifting the object of study, and hence very possibly failing to come to grips with the original problem; and any substantial gain in our understanding of them, changes them in ways which are often irreversible both factually and intellectually. We cannot become disintricated enough from them to dominate them as manipulable objects, and hence objectivity here has to mean something else; it can only mean that we come to put them in perspective.[23]

Such an understanding "may be very uncertain and fragmentary, and may be far from the coherent systematic interrelatedness which is the essense of reversibility."[24] But it may be more true. In morally ambiguous situations, the only true way to see things is ambiguously.

Formal reversible thinking is often required for a systematic articulation of the *justification* of mature moral judgments and actions insofar as they can be systematically justified. But it is not necessary for making those judgments and carrying out those actions. Contrary to Kohlberg, one need not be a moral philosopher in order to be a moral person. People who have a sufficient cognitive capacity for empathizing with the needs of others, the capacity to sustain a sense of the continuous identity of other persons, a capacity for imaginatively interpreting the nature and meaning of situations, and a sufficiently rich, imaginal repertoire by means of which to carry out such interpretations may be able to make extremely perceptive and fully moral judgments. Whether such psychological capacities are in fact actualized or not will depend on a number of other variables, including, perhaps, the extent of a person's experience with other, less fortunate people, the way one is socialized to handle feelings of distress over troublesome situations, and that indefinable quality of spirit to which Coles refers.[25]

The Operational Claim

Kohlberg's operational claim is that we can analyze the nature of a person's morality by looking at the pattern of judgments a person makes about situations in which people have conflictng claims on one another. This, he argues, will provide a gestalt of the structure of a person's moral stage. Now we are in a position to see why this claim, too, is false.

Roger Straughan has pointed out the inadequacy of using hypothetical moral dilemmas to find out much of anything about a person's morality. Because hypothetical dilemmas remove us from actual involvement in a situation, our answers to them cannot tell us anything about what we would actually do, or even what we would actually think, in a real situation.

> What seems to be lacking in the hypothetical presentation is precisely that feature which would make the real life situation a *moral* problem—immediacy. It is the immediacy of the inclination (not to get into trouble with the police) which I experience firsthand that *creates* the moral conflict; it is my own situational reasons, motives, wants and emotions which clash with the principle of truth-telling, and so face me with a moral decision to make. The actual motivational effect, though, of states of mind like fear, love, grief and awe cannot be properly appreciated secondhand.[26]

Another way of saying this is: Hypothetical dilemmas present a world that is an objective, reversible, manipulable world in which we are not involved as real selves. Such dilemmas have no way of presenting any other kind of world. If the real world were like that, this would not be a problem. We would be able to tell something from people's responses to hypothetical dilemmas. But, in fact, it is not—and that makes all the difference. The difference is not only in how we act, but also in how we see, think, feel, and understand.

An even more radical critique of the operational claim can be made, however. The use of hypothetical dilemmas is not the only thing that makes Kohlberg's claim questionable. Why should we concentrate on dilemmas at all? Not all of what constitutes one's morality consists of responding to problematic social situations. A person's morality cannot be summed up in the decisions one makes and the justifications one gives for those decisions. Most of what constitutes a person's morality refers to basic attitudes toward life and the underlying vision of reality that provides the foundation of those attitudes. A person's morality is an ongoing quality of life and not disjointed responses to isolated situations. When we ordinarily think about what makes people moral and what makes them morally different, we do not so much consider their decisions about particular moral dilemmas; rather,

> we consider something more elusive which may be called their total vision of life, as shown in their mode of speech or silence, their choice of words, their assessments of others, their conception of their own lives, what they think attractive or praise-worthy, what they think funny; in short, the configurations of thought which show continually in their reactions and conversation. These things, which may be overtly and comprehensively displayed or inwardly elaborated and guessed at, constitute what, making different points in two metaphors, one may call the texture of a man's being or the nature of his personal vision.[27]

The moral life, considered from this point of view, cannot be reduced to choices and justifications or scored in terms of stages.

Many people may not be fully conscious that they have a particular moral vision. If they are, they will not always be able to articulate it clearly or comprehensively. In any case, communication of one's moral vision or texture of being cannot be achieved by simply specifying what one sees the relevant facts to be in a clearly definable conflict of claims and by justifying how one chooses sides. It will instead involve the use of a nuanced moral vocabulary "betokening different ranges and ramifications of moral concept."[28] This vocabulary will include metaphors and stories full of subtle symbols and meanings that just any reasonable person cannot automatically be assumed to understand. "We differ," says Murdoch, "not only because we select different objects out of the same world but because we see different worlds."[29] It is very difficult, operationally, to become conscious of how our visions differ and to communicate them to or perceive them in others.

Our decisions and choices are rooted, however, in our visions of the world. Different visions lead to different choices. James McClendon, in his critique of "decisionism" (the tendency in moral philosophy to concentrate solely on dilemmas, decisions, and actions), points out that most of what appears outwardly in action and decision is a natural response to what we see going on rather than a result of conscious rational deliberation.

> Jesus, according to Matthew's judgment-parable of the sheep and the goats, tells his hearers that the actions by which their final destiny is judged are not the result of their deliberate choices, but are instead ones in which they act unknowingly, and yet showed themselves for what they truly were: it is "unconscious" acts of charity and mercy (or their absence) which are the true harbingers of our last estate, these and not our informed "decisions." (Matthew 25:31-45)[30]

And, as Murdoch points out, our responses in these "unconscious" moments depend on what our personal character or way of being enables us to see: "I can only choose within the world I can see, in the moral sense of 'see' which implies that clear vision is a result of moral imagination and moral effort. . . . One is often compelled almost automatically by what one can see."[31]

The displacement of decision and choice about isolated dilemmas from the center of our understanding of morality requires a different understanding of what a moral judgment is. Moral judgments are not exclusively, or even primarily, the judgments we make when we apply rules or principles to particular cases. Moral judgments also take the form of the descriptive-evaluative judgments we make constantly as we relate to people and situations in particular ways from our own points of view. "My employer is overbearing"; "She is a silly woman"; "This is an impossible situation"; "I really can't figure out why I get so angry every time I just see him"—these are moral judgments, too, and our most important ones. They are our evaluations of what is going on in the world. They are the basis on which most of our actions with regard to one another are made. Our moral judgments are the way we look at things. They have less to do with particular cases, decisions, and logical reasons than they do with our general moral vision and quality of perception. Moral judgments, understood in this way, can never be impersonal and abstract. They may become progressively more penetrating and realistic or progressively more shallow and delusional, but they never achieve completeness or perfection. The morality of our decisions depends on the adequacy of our descriptive evaluations. But the criterion for them is not a logical principle. It is the reality before us—which can never be fully known.

The upshot of all of this is that an analysis of deliberate choices is not, as Kohlberg claims, the best and only justifiable way of studying moral development. The study of people's morality and the way it changes will require a much more subtle examination of the full texture of their lives.

Religion and Morality

Kohlberg's theory of moral development does not have any explicit religious claims built into its internal structure. But he has spoken to religious groups concerning moral education and has had some things to say about the relation between religion and morality. Since his theories have had such a strong impact on religious educators' understanding of moral education, we need to take a look at where he stands on this issue.

In an early discussion, Kohlberg argued that religious belief and moral development are independent of one another. He claimed this largely on empirical grounds by citing some research findings: (1)

American subjects use very little religious language in responding to moral dilemmas and in justifying their responses; (2) in more religiously homogeneous societies religious language is used at the earlier developmental stages, but drops out in the postconventional stages; and (3) no differences in moral development have been found that are due to religious beliefs. From this Kohlberg concluded that the data provide "direct evidence against the view that the development of moral ideologies depends upon the teachings of particular religious systems," and that "religion is not a necessary or highly important condition for the development of moral judgment and conduct."[32]

In saying this, Kohlberg was not denying that life in the church may play a part in the development of morality. It simply has no unique part to play. Insofar as one gains social experience, undergoes cognitive conflict, is exposed to moral reasoning more adequate than one's own, and lives in a "just community" in the church, one's natural moral development can be stimulated there as well as anywhere else. But nothing special about the religious community makes this happen. The religious community offers no special advantage over other communities.

Kohlberg's more recent attempts to understand the relation of religious faith to the moral life do not substantially deviate from this earlier position. The core of the moral life is still the way we adjudicate conflicting claims, and our principles for doing this "can be defined and justified without reference to a specific religious tradition."[33] He does, however, suggest that moral development may parallel "faith development" as that is defined by James Fowler.[34] His proposal here is that the same cognitive structures that shape our perspective on moral decision making also shape our perspective on our relationship to God.

> At our moral Stage 1, divinity is bound to be an authority who is the ultimate dispenser of punishment and reward. At our moral Stage 2 one of our children says, "You be good to God and he will be good to you." The relation of man and God is one of exchange and trade. At moral Stage 3 the notion of divinity as moral ideal, as an ideally good

person, as the carer and protector of goodness is first entertained. At moral Stage 4 divinity is first seen as law-giver, bound by law and the ultimate ground of order. At moral Stage 5 divinity or the ultimate becomes identified with or is the ground of freedom, individuality and responsibility.[35]

The religious life, which Kohlberg confines to our conception of our relation to divinity, is seen as an application of the same structures of reasoning that we use in moral decision making to a cosmic level. For this reason, Kohlberg suggests that "development to a given moral stage precedes development to the parallel faith stage."[36] When we develop new cognitive structures, we develop them first in relation to that which is most immediate and concrete: first in terms of physical objects and logical reasoning, then in terms of social relations. Only when these patterns are fairly well stabilized are we able to use our cognitive structure to organize our relationship to the cosmos.

Kohlberg has a philosophical commitment that inclines him toward his view. He puts it this way: "Philosophically I incline toward Kant's solution, that faith is grounded on moral reason because moral reason 'requires' faith rather than that moral reason is grounded on faith."[37] This distinction is offered in order to preserve the radical autonomy of the institution of morality. If moral decision-making principles constitute morality, then morality cannot be grounded on faith because people's faiths differ. Grounding morality on faith would lead to relativism, either the relativism of social groups that claim a divine and authoritative text, or the relativism of the individual who claims a direct divine inspiration.

But, if morality is not grounded in faith, what is meant by the claim that moral reason "requires" faith? The answer to this question is given by Kohlberg's Stage 7. Stage 7 is not strictly a cognitive-structural stage, because it is not a single coherent logical system. Nor is it a moral stage in the sense that it defines a patterned process for adjudicating competing claims in situations of social conflict. Rather, it is "an ontological or religious" stage that integrates the universal human principles of justice with "a perspective on life's ultimate meaning."[38] Kohlberg connects this stage with the moral stages, because he contends that "ultimate moral maturity requires a mature solution to the question of the meaning of life."[39]

The major characteristic of all forms of Stage 7 (there can be a variety since it is not a purely logical structure) is an apprehension of cosmic unity in which one sees oneself to be a part of the whole. We come to see ourselves from the point of view of the infinite. Such an apprehension is often stated theistically, but it need not be. To show that this is so, Kohlberg cites the example of the Roman Emperor Marcus Aurelius, whose faith was in a lawful, rational universe to which he felt himself intimately related and to which he believed his own life could be entrusted.

Kohlberg does not tell us why we need to apprehend a cosmic intuition like this in order to be able to stick to our principles and thus become morally mature. Nor does he tell us how this apprehension accomplishes this task. There is good reason for this. For Kohlberg, religion consists mainly of a person's conception of the ultimate nature of reality. Religion is not concerned with a transcendent being quite other in nature from ourselves, mostly hidden, and ultimately an unfathomable but nonetheless active mystery. Nor is religion concerned with the particular images, rituals, symbols, stories, histories, and ways of living of particular religious communities and individuals. Instead, religion is, for him, our picture of divinity and the cosmos that divinity is believed to order. What appears in religion is simply a reflection of the ordering processes of our own cognitive structures. The cosmic intuition reveals nothing more than what is already implicitly given in our own structures of thinking. The reason Kohlberg cannot tell us why a cosmic intuition is necessary for moral maturity is that it isn't—at least not as an intuition different from or in addition to what we already tacitly assume.

Religious faith and belief have been collapsed here into human psychological structures. They no longer have as their real referent a reality that transcends, differs from, and has power independent from human consciousness. To say that moral reason requires faith turns out simply to mean that moral reason must be confirmed by the picture of the cosmos that one holds. Otherwise one's way of operating morally has no fundamental justification and is ultimately threatened by meaninglessness. Kohlberg's Stage 7 is the way the human self metaphorically projects such meaning out of its own consciousness, and this is what Kohlberg understands the nature and function of religion to be. This understanding of religion is Kantian in nature and quite consistent with the modern, humanistic reduction of transcendence to acts of human consciousness.

This conception has the advantage for Kohlberg of maintaining the primacy and autonomy of the moral domain. Since religious faith is ultimately only an extension of our cognitive moral structures onto a cosmic plane, faith development never really affects moral development and religious beliefs do not really shape moral judgments. The claim that "religion is not a necessary or highly important condition for the development of moral judgment" can, therefore, still stand. Development in the two domains is simply mutually confirming. In this way one's moral judgments are reinforced, but not altered or shaped, by faith.

If, however, religious faith has to do with the way in which people are related to a transcendent center of power and reality that is distinct from themselves and their own structures of consciousness, and that acts in the world and in themselves to convert their patterns of thinking and ways of living, then faith and morality may be more intimately and effectively related. Here religious faith is not a matter of being confirmed in what we already implicitly know, but of being moved to new ways of seeing, knowing, feeling, and relating. And this has everything to do with how we make moral judgments and decisions.

If this is true, though, what sense can we make of Kohlberg's empirical grounds for rejecting a relationship between morality and religion? Why do his studies show little if any empirical relationship between moral judgment and religious belief? There may be a number of reasons, but one of the most important is that the kinds of dilemmas he poses to study people's morality provide little opportunity for subjects to make sensitive use of religious language. His method of study pays no attention to the aspects of our lives where our religious sensibilities and beliefs would show up in morally relevant ways. He is not interested in "the texture of a man's being or the nature of his personal vision," so he simply does not ask. His dilemmas are so barren, his investigative questions so centered on decisions and justifications, and his subjects' involvement in the dilemmas so negligible that it would be surprising if any sense of a person's religious perspective and its connection with his or her morality were to appear. By defining morality the way he does, and by studying moral development in the manner that he does, Kohlberg blinds himself to what relation between religion and morality there might actually be.

The Development of Social Reasoning?

If these criticisms of Kohlberg's position are correct, it becomes apparent that he has not been able to give an adequate account of what it means to be moral, what is involved in the development of the moral life, or what it takes to discern moral maturity in ourselves or in others. But even if this is true, it seems obvious that Kohlberg has put his finger on something that is important in the shaping of our moral lives. Stages in reasoning about public social situations where explicit claims conflict seem to exist in the sense that there are consistent replications of Kohlberg's empirical studies up through the point defined by his first four stages. (There is, however, increasing disconfirmation of the empirical reality of the last two stages. Psychologists are unable to get replications of Kohlberg's data on Stage 5, and Stage 6 has dropped out of Kohlberg's own scoring manual.)

What Kohlberg has discovered can, I think, be called the stages in the development of social reasoning. By social reasoning I mean the ability to adjudicate explicit claims in situations of social conflict. The arenas of our lives where such conflicts most often arise are political or social policy situations. And Kohlberg has lately been calling the kind of education he advocates "civic education." From the point of view of the juridical moral philosophical tradition that Kohlberg represents, social reasoning of this kind *is* moral reasoning, and to engage in such reasoning is to be moral. This position is a historically respectable position that has many advocates. But it is not the only one.

In the alternative position, which we will consider next, social reasoning does have a place. But it is neither a necessary nor a sufficient conditon for moral virtue. It can be a very considerable asset in helping us to think through moral perplexities. It is a necessary ability for anyone who would engage in moral philosophy or Christian ethics; and no one would doubt that such work can be very helpful in illuminating our condition and circumstances and in solving the social problems we do face. But social reasoning by itself can be a force for good or evil. Which it is depends on a number of things that lie outside the range of what Kohlberg has so far been able to articulate. Because of this, Kohlberg's theory of moral development seems a helpful, but ultimately inadequate, foundation for building an approach to moral education in the religious context.

II ALTERNATIVE FOUNDATIONS

2
Fundamentals: Visional Ethics

There are many differences between a juridical approach to the moral life and a visional one. But the roots of these differences lie in the quite distinct pictures they have of the world and the human person. Two quotations from Iris Murdoch, the principal philosophical advocate of a visional approach, sum up the differences clearly. On the differences concerning the moral world, she says:

> There are people whose fundamental moral belief is that we all live in the same empirical and rationally comprehensible world and that morality is the adoption of universal and openly defensible rules of conduct. There are other people whose fundamental belief is that we live in a world whose mystery transcends us and that morality is the exploration of that mystery in so far as it concerns each individual.[1]

The alternatives concerning the picture of the human person in these two approaches are contained in this affirmation:

> We are not isolated free choosers, monarchs of all we survey, but benighted creatures sunk in a reality whose nature we are constantly and overwhelmingly tempted to deform by fantasy. Our current picture of freedom encourages a dream-like facility; whereas what we require is a renewed sense of the difficulty and complexity of the moral life and the opacity of persons.[2]

The juridical picture conceives of the world as intrinsically knowable through the rational powers potentially available to all of us as free persons in control of ourselves and our environment. The visional picture is one of a world shot through with mystery that is hidden from us as frightened and self-deceived persons, and that only a strenuous effort of moral imagination and deep discernment can begin to plumb.

These differences lie at the level of fundamental assumptions. They are not resolvable by abstract argument. Which assumptions one makes depends on the shape of one's own experience. The choice between them is a moral, even religious, choice. Our task in this chapter is not to argue for one over the other, but to describe in some detail what the visional picture looks like in opposition to the juridical. Readers will have to decide which picture more accords with reality as they have experienced it.

Problems and Mysteries

Earlier I characterized juridical ethics as a problem-solving ethic. Visional ethics might be described as a mystery-encountering ethic. When I use the term *mystery* here, I use it in a special way, not the one we ordinarily use in common speech. In ordinary usage a mystery is a baffling puzzle or riddle, a perplexing problem that no one seems to have the answer to. Mysteries in this sense have solutions. After a diligent search and some felicitous logical deductions, someone discovers the clue to the riddle, figures out the puzzle, and dispels the mystery. There are no loose ends. The case is closed, and everyone can now see what seemed so impossible to see at the outset. When intelligence, insight, and persistence are brought to bear, the mystery is a mystery no longer. Mystery, here, is the same thing as a problem, and mystery-encountering ethics turns out to be the same as problem-solving ethics.

I am using the term in quite a different way, one that is biblical in nature and connects it with the idea of revelation. George Hendry writes that a mystery in the New Testament sense is a mystery "not because it offers so little to our understanding, but because its superabundant wealth overwhelms our understanding."[3] Here a mystery is not a problem that goes away once figured out. Instead, mystery is an enduring reality that we know only through a glass darkly and never exhaustively. What we do apprehend is somehow disclosed or revealed to us. We receive our knowledge of mystery as a gift and cannot grasp it for ourselves through our own powers alone. We encounter mystery as it encounters us.

Gabriel Marcel makes the distinction between a problem and a mystery this way:

> A problem is something which I meet, which I find complete before me, but which I can therefore lay siege to and reduce. But a mystery is something in which I myself am involved. . . . A genuine problem is subject to an appropriate technique by the exercise of which it is defined; whereas a mystery, by definition, transcends every possible technique.[4]

What Marcel is saying by making the distinction in this way is similar to the distinction made by Charles Taylor concerning two kinds of objectivity.[5] Kohlberg's understanding of objectivity is one that requires that reality be a system of coherently reversible relationships, objects that can be logically and factually manipulated and exhaustively understood. Here reality is ultimately a set of problems. Taylor's alternative understanding of objectivity realizes that reality is not always open to reversible operations and that this is partially because we ourselves are so deeply involved in it. For Kohlberg, all moral difficulties can be resolved by the use of a technique, namely, his universal decision-making rule. But for Taylor such resolution is not always possible. We may only be able to see into the situation more deeply and come to live in it differently.

Marcel says two further things about mysteries and problems. First he notes, "It is no doubt always possible (logically and psychologically) to degrade a mystery so as to turn it into a problem. But this is a fundamentally vicious proceeding, whose springs might perhaps be discovered in a kind of corruption of the intelligence."[6] It is always possible to treat a reality as a problem though it is in fact a mystery. We do this by keeping that reality at a distance from ourselves, by refusing to encounter it in its fullness and depth, and by subjecting it to our own manipulative power. This is what the husband does to the wife in our earlier example; he turns her into an object. This, Marcel suggests, is a vicious proceeding.

The second thing Marcel notes has to do with the way in which we come to encounter mysteries.

> In this sphere everything seems to go on as if I found myself acting on an intuition which I possess without immediately knowing myself to possess it—an intuition which cannot be, strictly speaking, self-conscious and which can grasp itself only through modes of experience in which its image is reflected, and which it lights up by being thus reflected in them.[7]

Mysteries cannot be seized. They can only be given. They come as a gift to which we can only in some way respond—either by ignoring them, by reducing them, or by receiving them. Our encounters with them do not take place by our initiative. They approach us almost without our knowing. And our knowledge of them is not a direct knowledge. We know them by the way in which their presence is reflected in the way we think and feel and act.

This, I recognize, is all rather abstract at the moment. But what I want to suggest is that the moral world is a world of mystery, rather than a world of problems. People are mysteries, and being moral means treating them as such. Our world is a mystery, and being moral means encountering it that way. At the depth of being there is an Ultimate Mystery, and being moral means being properly related to that Mystery.

People as Mysteries

In order to carry out the kind of decision-making operation that juridical ethics suggests is central to the moral life, all we need to know about people is certain "facts." Who are the parties to this dispute? What are their claims on each other? What has happened here that brings them to make these claims? The answers to all of these questions are publicly available. Any rational, persistent third party can dig them out by asking the right questions. The morally relevant dimensions of the persons involved are the roles they play in the situation plus the rights they claim and the obligations they have with respect to it. Anyone could be in any of those roles, and it does not matter who in particular is involved.

But people are more than this, and our everyday moral relationships with them require that we recognize this. To see people only as "roles" with rights and duties is to see them as objects and to treat them as abstractions. They become mere problems for us. There is a good reason why we see and treat other people this way, though. It is fear. Real people cannot be controlled as problems can, and we become afraid when we begin to lose control over things.

> What is feared is history, real beings, and real change, whatever is contingent, messy, boundless, infinitely particular, and endlessly still to be explained. . . . [F]ear of contingency and history is a fear of the real existing messy modern world, full of real existing messy modern persons, with individual messy modern opinions of their own.[8]

Juridical ethics makes a virtue out of this fear and builds it right into its approach to morality. For visional ethics, this fear is a moral defect, and our moral task is to overcome it.

G.K. Chesterton has written: "Love desires personality; therefore love desires division. It is the instinct of Christianity to be glad that God has broken the universe into little pieces, because they are living pieces."[9] This saying is a bit shocking. We ordinarily believe that what makes life good and happy is the commonality we enjoy with other persons. Love, we think, is the achievement of a unity between souls. What we love, we suppose, is what we can understand and grasp, what is ordered in a way consistent with the order we hope for in ourselves. But it is the other way around. People are mysteries just by virtue of the fact that we cannot get them taped down, secured, and under control. There is always more to them than we can comprehend. People are realities whose "super-abundant wealth overwhelms our understanding." There are depths to them that, as we come to know them more fully, are opened up to us—often in surprising and delightful ways, but also at times in frightful and disorienting ways. In any case, it is just their uniqueness and fundamental particularity that makes people mysteries—and treasures. To love other persons, to treat them justly (that is, in accordance with who they really are), is to regard them as mysteries. Murdoch has said that love is nothing less than "the nonviolent apprehension of difference."[10] It is "the perception of individuals."[11]

Does regarding people as mysteries, as particular individuals distinct from ourselves and all others, make any difference in the way we act? It does. A story that Stanley Hauerwas, a moral theologian, tells about himself in relation to his father illustrates.

Hauerwas's family was a western frontier family, and life at home was characterized by hard work and craftsmanship. In such a social setting life with a gun was as natural as life with a car is for suburbanites. Hauerwas himself left his family behind when he went off to study philosophy and theology in universities and graduate schools. The longer he stayed away, the more different he became from the people he grew up with.

> Married to a woman my parents would always have difficulty understanding, I then made my way to Yale Divinity School. . . . During my second year in Divinity School, everytime we called home the primary news was about the gun on which my father was working. During the off months of the winter, my father had undertaken to build a deer rifle. That meant everything from boring the barrel, to setting the sight, and hand-carving the stock. I thought that was fine since it certainly had nothing to do with me.
>
> However, that summer my wife and I made our usual trip home and we had hardly entered the door when my father thrust the now complete gun into my hands. It was indeed a beautiful piece of craftsmanship. And I immediately allowed as such, but I was not content to stop there. Flushed with theories about the importance of truthfulness and the irrationality of our society's gun policy I said, "Of course you realize that it will not be long before we as a society are going to have to take all these things away from you people."
>
> Morally what I said still seems to me to be exactly right as a social policy. But that I made such a statement in that context surely is one of the lowest points of my "moral

development"... . For I simply was not morally mature
enough or skillful enough to know how to respond properly
when a precious gift was being made.

For what my father was saying, of course, was some-
day this will be yours and it will be a sign of how much I
have cared for you. But all I could see was a gun. In the
name of moral righteousness I callously rejected it. I hope
that now I would be able to say, "I recognize what this gun
means and I admire the workmanship that has gone into it.
I want you to know that I will always value it for that and I
will see that it is cared for in a manner that others can
appreciate its value."[12]

The change that takes place in Hauerwas from the time he
rather cruelly rebuffed his father to the time he was able to act
appropriately is a change of vision. In the first instance, he was not
able to see his father, that concrete, particular individual to whom he
was related as a son and for whom that gun meant something
important that was connected deeply to his own personal history and
ways of understanding. All Hauerwas could see was a gun and a
representative of that general class of people who are somehow not
wise enough to know that guns are bad. Later, what he came to see
was his father, that one unique man. When he was able to see him, he
was able both to give and to receive love.

This illustration may seem so personal as to suggest that the
idea of persons as mysteries has significance only for interpersonal
morality. But it is not confined to that arena. Whether we make the
effort to see persons as mysteries rather than as problems influences
our actions in the broader social and political realms as well. Our
society's treatment of black people and other minorities is as much a
result of a perception of them as members of a social class who
present a social problem as it is a question of civil rights. Indeed, the
two questions are intimately connected. What we do about public
education will depend to a large extent on whether we are ever able
to consider children as particular individuals with particular gifts
and potentialities, or as members of a herd who must be kept
occupied for a certain number of hours per day for society's conve-
nience.

People are mysteries because they are different and unique. They have a reality of their own that is independent of our control and is deep beyond our comprehension.[13] Attending to them as such makes a difference. As Murdoch says, "True vision occasions right conduct. . . . The more the separateness and differentness of other people is realized, and the fact seen that another man has needs and wishes as demanding as one's own, the harder it becomes to treat a person as a thing."[14]

The Reality of the Good

There are very few value words in juridical ethics. The main ones are "right" and "wrong." Kohlberg claims that questions about our ultimate aims as human beings, about the nature of the good life, about any ultimate reality that might give meaning and order to the world in which we live, about how we are to discriminate value, truth, and beauty from corruption and falsehood, are "beyond the scope of the sphere of morality."[15] What is alone important in juridical ethics is whether a particular act is right or wrong, justifiable or unjustifiable. When a word like "good" is used, it is used as a description that we give to evaluate human acts. It is not used as a symbol that points to a reality, "the Good," in the light of which we might know certain acts, persons, or things to be good. In this sense, "values which were previously in some sense inscribed in the heavens and guaranteed by God collapse into the human will. There is no transcendent reality."[16]

Such a view is not unpopular. No longer living in a religious world, we in our culture tend to live on one plane. There are no depths or heights, no realities beyond us. Everything must be understood in terms of human action and reason because, ultimately speaking, that is all there is. This view may be regarded as an achievement of the maturity, freedom and autonomy of the human race. But it need not be. It may be seen as a symptom of our culture's overly optimistic sense of its own power and of its hubris. In any case, visional ethics, whether of a religious or nonreligious variety, attempts to restore the classical idea that we live in a universe of value that cannot be reduced to empirical facts and the projections of human emotion and rational consciousness.

The belief that there are transcendent realities such as the Good makes a difference in morality. It suggests that there is an order to things and that we may make moral progress with respect to that order. The Good, as a transcendent reality, is not just any good. It is the ultimate Good, the criterion by which any goodness is known and evaluated. The idea of the Good is therefore intimately connected to the idea of perfection. Only the Good is perfect Good; any good that we know immanently, then, is known to be somehow lacking and is therefore to some degree improvable.

But the Good does more than just show us a lack. It also provides a direction toward which one may always move in order to progress morally. In so doing, it draws us out from where we are. Murdoch suggests that we can see this most clearly in the case of art.

> The true artist is obedient to a conception of perfection to which his work is constantly related and re-related in what seems an external manner. One may of course try to "incarnate" the idea of perfection by saying to oneself "I want to write like Shakespeare" or "I want to paint like Piero." But of course one knows that Shakespeare and Piero, though almost gods, are not gods, and that one has got to do the thing oneself alone and differently, and that beyond the details of craft and criticism there is only the magnetic non-representable idea of the good which remains not "empty" so much as mysterious.[17]

What guides the true artist is not a ready-made empirical example of good art or a principle that, if followed, will produce good art. Rather, it is a reality beyond technique, example, and convention that draws the artist out to better art. The same is true in morals.

The Good is a mysterious reality. It is mysterious in the sense that it can never be quite captured, fixed, or defined. It recedes beyond every attempt to specify it either in language or action. In this sense, it is like the sun. We cannot see it. But we do see things by its light. Its reality and presence are known indirectly—as Marcel said was true of all mysteries.

This last point helps us to understand the relationship between the Good as a reality and what was said about seeing persons as particulars. What we see in the light of the Good are particulars. The Good enables us to discriminate and make distinctions, to discern detail, complexity, and nuances of difference. As a good poet will use words to make discriminations that help us to see more clearly the detailed complexity of our life, so the good person is able, in the light of the Good, to attend and respond to the particularity of persons.

Jesus said, "Be ye perfect as your heavenly Father is perfect." In saying this, he shows us that we must be guided by the perfection of the goodness of God, who transcends us and who is mystery to us, if we are to know the direction in which we are to move. In the story of the rich young ruler, Jesus condemned the young man, not for what he had done that was good, but because he had not considered that lack in himself which perfect goodness would reveal and which, had he been able to respond, would have drawn him out from beyond where he was into new ways of acting and being.[18]

Perfect goodness is not the only mystery by which we may be guided in the moral life, however. The Bible knows of "the peace of God which passes all understanding," a righteousness that goes beyond all human righteousness, and a justice that is not just equal rights. There is a unity that is not just the absence of certain specifiable divisions, and above all there is a perfect love of God that goes beyond our experience of human love. All of these chart out for us the way in which we are to move as moral beings, though it is also clear that we can never this side of the Kingdom complete the course or even specify fully and precisely what completing the course would consist of. Such realities can, however, give us direction and help us to know what it means to make some progress.

Principalities and Powers

The idea that there are transcendent realities, ultimately mysterious, by which the moral life is to be guided is not uniquely a Christian concept. It is found in Plato and in much of classical philosophy. Murdoch holds the idea, though she is not herself a Christian. A Christian view adds something to all this. It is the suggestion that transcendent centers of value are not only somehow there to be contemplated; they are unified in one Person, an active Power. The Good is not only a value; it is a force. And not just *a* force, but the ultimate power over all others. The world is held in the hands of the One by whom all goodness is known and in whom, ultimately, all goodness is found. Our task as moral beings is to be appropriately related to, not just guided by, that center of power and value. Our task is to be obedient to God.

The world of juridical ethics is barren of any sense of the reality of transcendent power. It is, as Murdoch characterizes it, "a totality of ultimate simple facts which have no necessary connection with each other."[19] "There is only the ordinary world which is seen with ordinary vision."[20] There are no "principalities and powers"—overarching powers for good and for evil—that work in us and in the world and with which we have to deal as moral beings. What is good is a result of human will, intelligence, and effort. Moral evil is the result of human error. There is no grace that works in us. There is no evil that in any real sense grips us, and from which we must be saved. If we are to be saved from anything, it is simply from our own stupidity, and that can be done through better education and the full use of our rational capabilities.

Here, again, the juridical view is the more modern. We tend, for example, to treat evil as a problem rather than a mystery. We assume that there is some set of techniques for ridding the world of evil. By doing so, however, we lay ourselves open to a tendency to become both cynical and overly optimistic. Either way, we are being unrealistic; both are mechanisms of evasion. We become overly optimistic when we think we have the techniques to rid the world of evil. We become cynical when these techniques begin to fail. This does not mean that we are not to try to do everything within our power to resist evil and eliminate what suffering we can. We must do this. But we must not have too high a view of our own power. We will fail. Failure against evil and suffering will always be a part of life. And when we do fail, we must not run from it. We must accept it and endure it.

A common criticism of modern medical professionals is that they fear suffering and death, and therefore strive to deny it. They struggle with all their might to defeat it, and usually this is good. But when they cannot win, they often turn from it to find another battleground, leaving the suffering and dying patient isolated and alone. No diatribe against doctors is intended here. We all run from irremediable affliction when we see it. But this is just the point. By treating evil and suffering as a problem, we do not learn to face it for what it really is: a reality, a power, and a mystery.

The New Testament drama is one of a confrontation between principalities and powers. Jesus gave sight to the blind, healed the sick, and stilled the storm. He was also crucified. He refused to deal with the power of evil by ignoring it or running away from it. When he could not defeat it by obliterating it, he defeated it by accepting it, by taking it upon himself in its most extreme form on the cross.

We are not called on to bear the kind of evil that Jesus bore. We could not. It would kill us. But, because the Son has borne it, we know that even the greatest evil we are called on to accept cannot separate us from the love of God, a power of goodness that is for us and that cannot be defeated.

These notions, that there are principalities and powers and that the drama we believe in shows how they are related, turn all our natural values topsy-turvy. There is no justice in the sense of equal rights in the cross; yet we are called to bear it. There is no happiness as we ordinarily understand it in accepting suffering about which we can do nothing; yet we are called to remain in it. There is no utility in trusting an ultimate Goodness we cannot see or comprehend; yet we are called to do so. But the promise is that in doing these things, we will encounter the world as it is in a way that we could not conceive on our own, and cannot conceive so long as we turn from or reduce these mysteries to something we can handle. In encountering these mysteries, we see more clearly who we are and what we ought to do. This, at least, is the promise of the Gospel and the testimony of the Church.

Sin and Sight

If we really do live in a world that is shot through with mystery, and if the moral life involves first and fundamentally coming to see this world as it is and to respond to it appropriately, then we must say something about what it takes to do so. At first glance, it would not seem to take much. Do we not all see the world every day? And do we not all respond in one way or another to what we see? What more can be involved in seeing than just looking? The fact is, however, that we do not see the world very clearly at all. Most of what we see is distorted and illusory. It is very difficult even to know that we see through distorted lenses. It is still more difficult to see rightly. As Murdoch says:

> By opening our eyes we do not necessarily see what confronts us. We are anxiety-ridden animals. Our minds are continually active, fabricating an anxious, usually self-preoccupied, often falsifying veil which partially conceals the world.[21]

The theological name for this inability to see rightly is sin. One of the great differences between visional ethics and juridical ethics is that the latter does not take sin very seriously at all. It pictures moral difficulties to be difficulties of thinking rationally, and suggests that moral progress is attainable by a combination of increased reasoning power plus sincerity or strength of will. But this, empirically, is not the case. People, as they strive to be moral, consistently find it impossible to think their way into goodness. Reasoning power plus willpower does not translate directly into moral power. Intuitively, we all know this to be true. We have all been in situations in which right reasoning did not bring about the discernment we needed, and we were as a result immobilized—for reasons that penetrate deeply into our personalities, needs, fears, desires, and self-protectiveness.

The controlling idea in juridical moral philosophy is that the structures of human reason are the sole means to the organization of the moral life. There is no essential breach between human beings and the mystery of the world. The rational mind makes an adequate bridge. But this rather optimistic view of the self is itself a delusion. In our least self-protective moments, we recognize this. The experience can be terrifying.

In Walker Percy's novel *Love in the Ruins,* a world very much like our world is pictured. There is rapid social change, values are in upheaval, men and women have difficulty knowing who they are and how to relate to one another. Physical violence runs rampant in society, and a kind of spiritual violence cuts a deep river at a more subterranean level. It becomes well-nigh impossible to love and care at all. Imbedded in all this himself, the hero of the novel, a psychia-

self - establishment

trist who has managed to invent a rather fanciful machine that measures human souls, reflects on the terror under which nearly everyone seems to suffer:

> Where did the terror come from? Not from the violence: violence gives release from terror. . . . No, the terror comes from the goodness and what lies beneath, some fault in the soul's terrain so deep that all is well on top, evil grins like good, but something shears and tears deep down and the very ground stirs beneath one's feet. . . . The terror comes from piteousness, from good gone wrong and not knowing it.[22]

Good does go wrong, and we are often unaware. The breach is there, and we call it sin. Can we understand anything about how it works?

The human self is very fragile. It is threatened on all sides. We know ourselves to be mortal creatures whose lives have only a short span, and whose most cherished plans are continually subject to disruption by chance and the limitations of our own finitude. We all need to make some sense of our lives, yet that sense seems continually undercut. We need our lives to be justified, but there seems no ultimate justification. We need to find our lives established on firm ground, but the ground gives way. We need to be sustained, but we cannot sustain ourselves. Our very mortality and finitude make us anxious. How can the anxiety be overcome? How can our lives be established and sustained?

Anxiety is overcome and our lives are established and sustained when we are noticed. Our lives are granted foundations when our being is reflected in the eyes of another. Children first come to know that they exist by being noticed. If children are not noticed, if their presence is not felt by others, their being is not secured and the formation of a secure sense of self is impossible. The need for the establishment and sustainment of the self is given with our existence. This need causes a fundamental insecurity that can be alleviated only by a sense that one is profoundly and permanently noticed by another. To receive such attention from one's parents when one is very young is to learn that one is accepted, valuable, and indispensable in the world. It is to learn that you are.

But note what happens when this certainty breaks down or fails to take hold. In this case, we begin to extend our presence, make our presence felt on others. We begin to use other people as mirrors within which to see ourselves reflected. We begin to manipulate others into responding to us. This process starts at a very young age, but it continues through life. In extreme cases, the process can result in severe neurosis. But it is our common condition. We all grow up. The security that was established for us by our parents and by our lack of awareness of the dangers of the world always breaks down. We move out into a wider world, conditions around us begin to change, and we come to realize that the sources of our former security are no more eternal and omnipotent than we are. Then the anxiety we only unconsciously felt as infants becomes more conscious. As its dimensions enlarge, we strive to deny the reality behind it and fabricate ways of making it go away.

The importance of this for the moral life is what it makes happen in our relationship with other people. When we take on the task of establishing and sustaining ourselves by making others take notice of us, we sense unconsciously that we must do so by making other persons into objects we can control.

From the very fact that I treat the other person merely as a means of resonance or an amplifier, I tend to consider him as a sort of apparatus which I can, or think I can, manipulate, or of which I can dispose at will. I form my own idea of him and, strangely enough, this idea can become a substitute for the real person, a shadow to which I shall come to refer my acts and words.[23]

The very process of self-establishment separates us from realistic relationships with others and from seeing them as they really are. By this means the "falsifying veil which partially conceals the world" is raised. We begin to see other people in terms of what we need or desire them to be. A teenage child is "impertinent" because he ridicules some of my most cherished notions. A colleague is "hateful" because she does not give me the deference I feel I am due. We see what we need to see in order to protect our fragile selves, and end up not seeing what is really there. The result of our seeing is to act in response to what we see. If my child is impertinent, I punish him. If my colleague is hateful, I refuse to listen to anything she has to say and block her promotion.

But it is not only other people who are seen falsely. Evidence is distorted in a cost-benefit analysis of nuclear power plants, because the people doing the study have too much economically at stake. Abortion becomes contraception when we are no longer able to care for children. A military attack becomes a defensive reaction when we are not able to see our nation as capable of wicked self-interest. All of these deceptions often happen quite unconsciously. It would be too threatening to make them conscious. In the process, even our language becomes double-talk and babble. Extraordinary discernment or a rude shock is required if we are to discover our deceptions at all.

Sadly, the whole process ends up being self-defeating. The security of self we seek to achieve is ephemeral, because it is not rooted in reality. As the process continues, we become decreasingly rather than increasingly secure, and our defenses take on more extreme dimensions. There is then no end to our ever more desperate attempts to put ourselves at the center of attention of the moral universe and no limit to the actions we will take to do it.

This protrusion of the self, this placing of the self at the center while holding all else in orbit around it, is what Marcel calls "the illusion of moral egocentricity."[24] It is a natural and persistent tendency that all of us have to one degree or another, and it can never be entirely eradicated. We certainly cannot simply, by being more rational, think ourselves out of this condition. The cause is too deep, and rationality cannot provide the cure.

> In fact, just as any notions we may have of cosmography do not rid us from the immediate impression that the sun and stars go round the earth, so it is not possible for us to escape completely here below from the preconceived idea which makes each one tend to establish himself as the centre around which all the rest have no other function but to gravitate.[25]

There are, however, degrees of moral egocentricity. Some people are more firmly captured by this illusion than others; some are able to pierce the veil to some extent and to see more clearly and realistically. Moral people are people who can see and do see. They have achieved some freedom from the captivity of egocentricity (this is the real meaning of moral freedom), and are therefore able to act as morally mature individuals. How does this happen?

There are moral, educational, and experiential answers to this question. It is partly a result of "a patient and just discernment and exploration of what confronts one, which is the result . . . of a . . . kind of moral discipline."[26] It is partly the result of being shown what is true by a morally good person who can use a language with us that will help us look closely at what we have not been able to see before. It may be the result of rudely shocking or surprisingly wonderful experiences that shake up our patterns of perception and make the old ones henceforth untenable. These answers are all important and will always be fundamental to moral growth. But, because the problem is sin and because its source has to do with our fundamental condition in human existence, the root answer is a religious one.

Our sinfulness arises out of an attempt on our part to guarantee that a real need of ours is met—to be noticed and loved for the unique, particular, mysterious being each of us is. That need cannot be wished away; it must be met. The dynamic of sin is broken only if we are in fact profoundly and permanently noticed and loved. One of God's greatest blessings is the love and attention we receive from other people, especially love and attention that we do not have to ask for and that we sense is love for us just as we are. But, because we are all sinners and all finite, none of us can be the source of permanent establishment and sustenance for another. We find out that, as much as we might like them to be, other people are not perfect, omnipotent, or eternal. They fail us on the one hand, and they die on the other.

That is why our release from sin, and hence our release from our egocentricity and the immoral character of our relations with each other, depends on God and on faith in God. Unless there is this reality that does in fact establish and sustain us by noticing us in love, permanently and utterly, our deepest need can never be fulfilled and we are on our own to try to meet it as best we can. If there is such a God, an adequate means for feeding this spiritual hunger is

sinfulness
from
human,
real need

available; we have only to recognize it. Faith, in this sense, is the deep, almost somatic conviction that we are loved and noticed by the ultimate Mystery as particular individuals. On the basis of this conviction, our distorting and destructive egocentricity can progressively be given up, and we can become more free to join the world as it is. In this sense at least, morality depends on religious faith.

Vision and Character

Kohlberg's juridical ethics scorns the notion of character. For him, character is a kind of disconnected "bag of virtues" or collection of "traits." He perceives no center of moral consistency within the human self except the patterned processes (structures) we have for processing information and connecting events in terms of fairness. He says, "The objection of the psychologist to the bag of virtues is that there are no such things."[27]

There probably is no such thing as a bag of virtues, but this does not mean that there is no such thing as character or that character is not a very important matter for the moral life. People are unitary beings, and not a cluster of separate, unrelated faculties. The name we give to this unity and the style we have of living as unified beings is character.

Character is very much connected with vision. In the first place, it is a fact of life that what we see depends not only on what is in front of our eyes, but also on what lies within our hearts and minds. Who we are determines what we see. Paul Holmer, in his study of C.S. Lewis, comments on Lewis's concern with vision:

> "Seeing" is not automatic, neither is hearing or feeling or thinking. The subject behind the activity will limit or extend the possibilities, depending upon what and who he or she is.[28]

> The world's infinite riches, its values and worths, its pleasures and depths can be found only if we are qualified subjects.[29]

What people see is an indication of what they care about and can care about. It is an indication of the depth and breadth of their compassion, of the scope and quality of their loves and desires, and of the intensity with which they feel. Our emotions, evaluations, descriptions, predispositions, and desires are all brought to bear in our seeing. Attention is the concentration of the whole self in a moment of time. The quality of that attention is largely determined by the quality of the self who attends.

But that is not all. The quality of our lives is, in turn, shaped by what we see. Acts of attention do not leave us unchanged. Each new act of attention broadens not only our world, but also our capacity to see deeply into that world. When other people or things or ideas are received by us through our realistic perception of them, we are not left as we were. When we fail to look, we lose the opportunity to be changed by what the object of our attention—"by being in its totality precisely the thing it is"[30]—can do to us. Paul instructs us to fill our minds with the things that are true, honorable, just, pure, lovely, and gracious, because he knows the power these things have to do their work in us.[31]

The Self as Story

The heading for this section is borrowed from the title of an essay by Hauerwas.[32] In that essay, Hauerwas suggests that the coherence of our moral lives, our character, is tied together with our ways of seeing in a manner that has storylike qualities. Who we are morally cannot be seen by the way we apply certain rather impersonal cognitive structures to isolated, unconnected situations.

> Rather, we exhibit an orientation that gives our life a theme through which the variety of what we do and do not do can be scored. To be agents at all requires a directionality that involves the development of character and virtue. Our character is the result of our sustained attention to the world that gives a coherence to our intentionality. Such attention is formed and given content by the stories

through which we have learned to form the story of our lives. To be moral persons is to allow stories to be told through us so that our manifold activities gain a coherence that allows us to claim them for our own. The significance of stories is the significance of character for the moral life as our experience itself, if it is to be coherent, is but an incipient story.[33]

We are not choosing-acting machines that produce decisions when social conflicts arise. We are dramas that have a past and a future. What we do and think in the present is our way of making sense of that past and the living toward the future we, perhaps obscurely, intend. To have character is to have—in a sense, to be—such a drama. To be of good character is to have and to be a story that makes sense in the light of what the world is really like.

The story that constitutes my character is not just a story that I tell about myself. It is the story that shines through my life. It is the story that my life tells. In fact, it is possible for me to tell stories about myself that are false. I may, out of fear or anxiety, tell stories of a kind that attempt to hide who I really am. If I am at some level partially aware of this, I will feel a certain tension in telling stories like this—though I may not know where that tension comes from. If I am thoroughly self-deceived, I may not even notice that some of my stories are artificial. Other people who are morally discerning will sense, however, that something is not quite right. They will notice that my stories do not ring true. My false stories will then be a sign to them of a fault in my character, or even a sign that to a degree I lack character.

My honest story, the one that really forms my character, will be one made up of my most fundamental convictions. Convictions are beliefs. They are our beliefs about what the world is like, about who we are, about what things are most important. But they are not just beliefs about things. They are "those tenacious beliefs which when held give definiteness to the character of a person or of a community, so that if they were surrendered, the person or community would be significantly changed."[34] A conviction is something we cannot help believing because, if we did not believe it, we would not be ourselves anymore. In this way, we can almost say we *are* our convictions. Our convictions tell us who we are. As we live, we reveal by our living our convictions to others. And others who know us well know what is significant and persistent in us.

Persistence and significance are two marks of convictions.[35] Convictions are persistent in that they are not easy to change. They have the capacity to resist attack, to overcome, and to continue in the face of difficulties and threatening circumstances. They are significant, because they are organizing beliefs. They make sense of the rest of our beliefs. They are the beliefs that guide us in our acting and seeing—especially our spontaneous, prereflective, habitual ways of seeing and acting.

This, of course, does not mean that convictions or character is irrational. Persons of conviction and character are usually people who have given thoughtful consideration to their most fundamental beliefs, have tested them in their own experience and against the experience and thought of others, and have striven for a coherence between what they believe and the demands of reason. But the rationality of conviction is not an abstract, impersonal rationality that is primarily expressed in propositions. Rather, it is the kind of rationality that is imbedded in and expressed through a good story. A good story is meaningful, connected, and coherent. But it is not propositional. What happens next cannot be *deduced* from what happened first, though what happens next must follow narratively from what happened first. Narratives make a point, and a rational point—but not just a logical point. The point of a story is "a connection among elements (actions, events, situations) which is neither one of logical consequence nor one of mere sequence. The connection seems rather designed to move our understanding . . . forward by developing or unfolding it."[36]

Indeed, if I wish to say something meaningful about my convictions to someone, I will find that just stating my beliefs does not communicate much. Sooner or later I will find myself virtually compelled to tell a story, a story that somehow reveals something important about myself. It may be a story about how I lived through some terrible times, and could not find any way out; and how I struggled and struggled and then finally just gave up in defeat; and how then and only then things seemed to fall into place through no extra effort on my part; and how I felt relieved of a burden that had in some inexplicable way been lifted from me. Or it might be about a time when I was forgiven when I had no right to be, but was anyway. It is by telling such stories that we explain and communicate our convictions, and hence our characters or our selves.

Although stories that reveal character can often be short stories that focus on one or a few important occasions, the full stories of our lives are long and complex. We are historical beings to whom and in whom many things have happened. Life stories pick up many of the details of this history and place them in relation to one another. Such stories are not, however, merely chronicles that become more complete when more items are added. They are interpretations. They pull in the past in ways that give that past some sense and meaning that can be understood in the light of the present and intended future. Hauerwas does this when he tells the story about the incident with his father. His story is not just about an occurrence that took place. He tells us about a part of his life in a way that shows how he now understands the whole of his life in a particular way. He does this because he wants us to understand his life in the same way. By telling that story in that particular way, Hauerwas means to show us something of who he is now.

Life stories change. Though they are persistent, like the convictions that are part of them are persistent, they are not rigid. Our stories change, our convictions and character change, when and because we change. Something new happens that makes a crucial difference in our lives: a devastating illness, the death of a loved one, an experience of undreamt joy, a new friend, an important and revolutionary new idea. In response to such experiences, we become different and our stories need to be reworked. Earlier experiences that we thought insignificant now take on special meaning. Beliefs once held sacred are now shaken. The story is now a different story. It is not discontinuous with the old one, but a new one that incorporates the old one in it.

Stories of this kind are not abstract. They are particular. They are made up of particular incidents, characters, settings, images, metaphors, and beliefs. Our fathers and mothers, sisters and brothers, friends and enemies are all involved. So are the particular ideas, words, rituals, tales, and rules that we get from other people in our

social setting and adopt as our own. Our life stories are not purely
private; nor are they isolated from the life stories of others and of the
communities in which we live. Our own stories and character share
much in common with those of others. We grow by learning, and not
just by developing what is already there within. It matters where we
live, whom we learn from, and what the convictions and stories of
our communities are.

Character and Community

Communities are not just aggregates of individuals whose rights
and duties bounce off of each other like billiard balls. Communities
are organic bodies of people who are intersubjectively related to one
another as mysteries, and who hold convictions, stories, and visions
in common. Communities can have character, too. The character of
a community shapes the character of its people. It does this in several
ways.

First, communities have historical dramas of their own that, as I
become a member of that community, I come to adopt as part of my
own drama. The story of the founding of the community becomes
part of my own story. Great events that most clearly illuminate the
character of the community become events in my own history. But it
is not just the past drama that becomes part of my drama. As a
current member of the community, I play a part in the continuing
drama and intermesh my story with the ongoing story of the community. Some members of the community make such an impact on it
that they to some degree change the character of the community,
and their stories become an occasion and impetus for the community's story to be rewritten.

Second, communities have convictions and ways of seeing that
also become my own. Indeed, I cannot really be a member of a
particular community unless I share the community's most fundamental convictions. We may not always agree with the ways in
which they are expressed. We may find ourselves going through
years of struggle over their meaning and roots in reality, a period
that always seems to involve profound doubt and intensive criticism.
We may even feel we have rejected them, only to find later that at a

deeper level they were shaping us all the while. In all of these cases, the convictions of the community frame our quest. We really leave a community only when we leave the quest that its convictions shape.

Dag Hammarskjöld, the former secretary-general of the United Nations, provides an example of this. He was raised in a religious family, which held convictions that marked him for life. His diary, *Markings,* reveals an intensive struggle with those convictions, with the meaning of his life, and with the shape of his own character. After nearly thirty years, however, when the struggle somehow ceased and he felt he had broken through into maturity, he came to accept these convictions in his own way.

> When I finally reached that point, the beliefs in which I was brought up and which, in fact, had given my life direction even while my intellect still challenged their validity, were recognized by me as mine in their own right and by my free choice. I feel that I can endorse those convictions without any compromise with the demands of that intellectual honesty which is the very key to maturity of mind.[37]

Third, communities have languages and rituals of their own that both show forth and shape their visions. Particularly important here are the key images and metaphors and symbolic actions that give a community's language and rituals their particular distinctiveness. The actions of the business community are shaped by a language dominated by "profits," "losses," "returns on investments," "capital goods," and so forth. Its rituals include promotions, annual meetings, retirements, and mergers. It is impossible to become a part of the business community without using this language and participating in these rituals. But once one is in this community it is very hard to see what is going on around one in any other terms. It is almost impossible, for example, for some corporate managers to see the distribution of infant formulas in poverty-stricken areas as anything other than simply "advertising" a "viable product" and "providing services" in order to "return a profit." All communities have a language system that reflects and shapes their character and the character of their members. The question is, does the language picture the world as it is?

Communities are not just symbol and belief systems, however. They are active bodies that act on individuals and call individuals into action. So the fourth way in which communities are important for character has to do with the effects of their action. Some communities treat their members and others primarily as objects. When this is true, the members become frightened and insecure. In order to protect themselves, they, in turn, treat others as objects, and a vicious cycle feeds on itself. Other communities are able to treat people as mysteries. Such treatment has a freeing effect. Because I know that I am, at least to some extent, recognized for who I am, I may allow my defenses to drop a bit. Then I can see others more as they are.

Moral communities may do more than just free me from ego-centric self-defense, however. They may also show me what I am not yet able to see on my own. Such communities may involve me in activities that I would fear on my own. They may bring me up short against what I refuse to admit, and jar me back into reality. In sum, they may broaden and deepen my world by involving me in it in ways that I might otherwise positively flee.

8 - strength

The importance of the church for the moral life is not just the fact that it might provide an arena for social role-taking. Its importance lies in its character as a particular community that holds particular convictions, stories, language, rituals, and forms of action in common. The church, through its scripture, tradition, and theology, provides a history and a moral and spiritual vocabulary. Among its crucial events are the Exodus; the rise and fall of Jerusalem; the birth, life, death, and resurrection of Jesus of Nazareth; Pentecost; Augustine's conversion; Luther's nailing of ninety-five theses on the Wittenberg door; and Martin Luther King's advocacy of civil rights. We become children of Abraham, disciples of Jesus Christ, and brothers and sisters of all humanity. We take bread and wine, and are washed in water. We confess our sins and receive forgiveness. We see Jesus feeding thousands, healing lepers, eating with sinners, and hanging on the cross. We know that it is harder for rich people to enter the Kingdom of Heaven than it is for the camel to go through the eye of a needle. We have heard the story of workers who came late but received as much as those who labored from early morning. Hauerwas says that

> our attending cannot be separated from the language or metaphors which form it. If these metaphors do not help us to "see" the world as it is ... they should be given up. But the claim of the Christian is that his language actually envisages the world as it is.[38]

If this is true, then the incorporation of this vocabulary and these rituals, stories, metaphors, and images into our own ways of thinking, understanding, feeling, intending, and perceiving will shape our character in such a way that we will be able more accurately to pay attention to *reality*, and be less likely to flee into our own social and personal dream worlds.

The church is a living and acting community. Through its pastoral care and prophetic action, the church strives to attend to persons as particulars and to move its people into the world in ways we would often prefer to ignore or escape. It points our perception toward realities we could not otherwise see, and helps us to see more deeply into what we have taken for only surface realities. It is a community of moral discourse and action that opens us, encourages us, judges us, and challenges us.

That the church often fails in these tasks is all too obvious to everyone. As a community, its vision is often distorted, its language obscuring rather than clarifying, and its action self-protective and unresponsive. But as a community, the church is characterized by its knowledge of itself as a community of sinners and it continues daily to confess that. Furthermore, it relies on a Power that is not its own and knows that it can do nothing and see nothing by its own efforts. Such a self-image is in itself realistic, and is a foundation for moral growth.

Responsible Action

One of the things we wish for from ethics is that it will help us to know how we should act. The focus, in juridical ethics, on the decisions and choices we make or recommend that others make in particular situations gives that form of ethics its initial appeal. It purports to provide a clear guide for action through its rules and principles for decision making. In juridical ethics, prescribed action follows directly from the application of principles to case, and all that is required from us is the power of will.

The help that visional ethics provides in this area is much less direct. Decisions, choices, and particular actions are not the first consideration in visional ethics. The foreground is occupied by questions concerning what we see and what it is that enables human beings to see more realistically. For visional ethics, action follows vision; and vision depends on character—a person thinking, reasoning, believing, feeling, willing, and acting as a whole. In this context, the place of choices, decisions, and actions is a different one. Their sources and justifications are not abstract, impersonal, universal principles, but "a trained relentlessness in viewing the realities of life"[39] that issues from the quality of consciousness and character of particular moral persons and communities.[40]

This means that visional ethics cannot provide a measuring stick by which to evaluate action from a point of view that is disinterested and uninvolved in the ongoing lives and contexts that give rise to the difficulties we have. It cannot answer in the abstract the question, "What is the right thing to do?" The help it provides instead is the help that comes when someone describes the world clearly for us, tells stories and uses images and metaphors that help us to see what is there, and clarifies for us what we are up against in ourselves and in the world in trying to see for ourselves. Visional ethics invites us to look, and attempts to frame our vision and teach us to see.

Theoretically, this is one of the frustrating aspects of visional ethics. We really do want a measuring stick. We want to be relieved of the hard, inconclusive, exhaustingly concrete and complex work of looking closely, and of the responsibility for our own being and acting that is placed on us. Practically, however, this approach to ethics is more helpful and more realistic. If you have ever tried to help people who were struggling to decide whether or not to have an abortion, whether or not to resist the draft, how to take care of their elderly parents, how to deal with their retarded child, whether or not to support a particular candidate for public office, or any of the infinite number of moral quandaries people have, you know that rules and measuring sticks do not really provide adequate help. We have to be with people, think with people, and help them to see and feel themselves deeply and realistically through their struggles. When we do this, we are trying to help them respond appropriately to the reality that lies before them and within them. We are trying to help them act "fittingly" or "responsibly."

These last two terms are taken from H.Richard Niebuhr, whose ethic of responsibility is a form of visional ethics. There are four fundamental ideas at the foundation of responsibility that pull together a number of the themes with which we have been dealing and that, compositely, describe the nature of responsible action: response, interpretation, accountability, and community solidarity.[41]

All of our actions are *responses* to what is going on in the world. We do not "intercede" in it from above; we are deeply imbedded in it, and our actions are part of its ongoing, intricate, dynamic history. Our responses, however, are not naked reflexes to raw incidents. Responses are actions done in the light of meaningful events. Our actions are responses to realities that are already full of meaning because of the *interpretations* that our seeing brings. Niebuhr says,

> We are characterized by awareness and . . . this awareness is more or less that of an intelligence which identifies, compares, analyzes, and relates events so that they come to us not as brute actions, but as understood and having meaning.[42]

We respond, in other words, to an already interpreted reality. We act in accordance with what we see. Part of our task, then, as moral beings is to see well and to interpret truthfully. "In our responsibility we attempt to answer the question: 'What shall I do?' by raising as the prior question: 'What is going on?' "[43]

Accountability refers to the way in which the actions of a responsible person not only respond to a past but also fit into an anticipated future. The responsible self is one who "stays with his action, who accepts the consequences in the form of reactions and looks forward in a present deed to the continued interaction."[44] The responsible person, in other words, is one whose action is part of a drama or story. Indeed, accountable action is action that shapes living stories, both the self's own story and the stories of others.

Responsible stories are those that foster *social solidarity.* The responsible self is responsible for living in, learning from, and helping to shape community. "Personal responsibility implies the continuity of a self with a relatively consistent scheme of interpretations of what it is reacting to. By the same token it implies continuity in the community of agents to which response is being made."[45] The responsible self is possible only when there are responsible communities that try to see the world as it is and express what they see in languages, rituals, and patterns of living that reveal rather than conceal it. People learn to be responsible by living in such communities, and by taking responsibility for making fitting contributions to them.

An ethic that does not aid us in our action is not an ethic worth pursuing. But our actions are not isolated applications of rational principles to discrete cases. They are ongoing responses to what we see, and these depend on what we can see. To act fittingly and responsibly is to act in response to truthful seeing, a seeing that peers into the mysterious depths of the world and requires long discipline, patient effort, and the continuous shaping of the whole self by what is real.

Implications

If the moral life is anything like what I have described, the implications are far-reaching. In moral psychology, it will not be enough to investigate the development of cognitive structures. The dynamics of self-deception and self-protectiveness, on the one hand, and of trust, receptivity, and discernment, on the other, will have to be explored. We will need some clues as to how language and ritual and life-in-community shape us. A psychology of character will need to be developed in which the roots of a coherence of vision, thought, feeling, and action can be discovered, and the dynamics of change charted out.

Moral education will also be different. Its aim will not just be to help people develop their innate capacities to reason in situations of social conflict. Rather, it will need to strive for the formation of character and the fostering of communities in which people learn to see deeply into the mysteries of the world and to respond to that vision responsibly. It will involve the teaching of a language and a way of living that put us in contact with the world, and that are shaped by the heritage and vision of particular communities.

Finally, there will be a difference in how we go about assessing people's morality. Rather than giving them a test and scoring their stage, we will need to learn to listen to the stories they have to tell about themselves, relate them to the stories that shine through in their living, and look to see how each illuminates the other. In short, we will have to pay a great deal of attention to people. There are no shortcuts.

3
Dynamics: Imagination
and Revelation

We have become increasingly accustomed to identifying moral growth or moral progress with "moral development." We assume almost automatically that, if we grow morally or mature morally, this must mean we have developed morally. Such a substitution of terms would be no problem except for the fact that the word "develop" has taken on special meaning because of its use in the context of "developmental" psychology. In this context, development has increasingly come to imply movement through stages of one kind or another. As a result, it is almost second nature to us now to wonder what stage we are in when we think about our own moral lives. And when a new theory is put forward, one of the first things we want to know about it is the stages of development it describes and how these compare with Kohlberg's or Piaget's.

While all this talk about development and stages has been helpful in focusing our attention on some important aspects of the movement of human beings toward greater moral maturity, it has at the same time blinded us to other features that are just as important.

The first of these is the significance of particular experiences. Many of us have had personal, often private, experiences at times in our lives that provide for us a key by which the rest of life is interpreted and an anchor to which our actions are attached. Often these experiences come in times of suffering or testing. We come up against hard times, and in them find out what our resources are and who we are in relation to others. Though we know of such experiences and their critical significance in our own lives and the lives of others very close to us, they are mostly hidden. Nonetheless, such experiences are often occasions in which we give a fundamental answer to the questions our lives ask us. We begin to write the stories that our lives will tell, and who we are morally is very much a part of these stories.

An example of this is found in Jacques Lusseyran's autobiography, *And There Was Light.* Lusseyran tells the story of how he was able to live out of the strengths he found at the age of seven when he was blinded in a school accident. Lusseyran, unlike a neighbor child who was similarly disabled at about the same age, was able with the help of his parents to accept the fact of his blindness and to live his life graciously and intensively out of a light he even then sensed moving through him. He says of himself:

> Every day since then I have thanked heaven for making me blind while I was still a child not quite eight years old.
>
> . . . The habits of a boy of eight are not yet formed, either in body or mind. His body is infinitely supple, capable of making just the movement the situation calls for and no other; ready to settle with life as it is, ready to say yes to it.
>
> . . . I know that since the day I went blind I have never been unhappy.[1]

At the age of nineteen, held at Buchenwald, the Nazi concentration camp, for his activities in the French resistance, what he experienced as a child could be passed on to others. He was able to help his fellow-prisoners to "go about holding on to life. I could turn towards them the flow of light which had grown so abundant in me. . . . Often my comrades would wake me up in the night and take me to comfort someone, sometimes a long way off in another block."[2] Lusseyran's answer of yes to life in his childhood experience of being blinded was the foundation of his moral life.

Not everyone has had experiences that are so profound and determinative as Lusseyran's.[3] But each of us has had experiences we recognize as keys to the quality and character of our own particular moral lives. It may be an experience of having done something shockingly wrong—or shockingly right—that made you see yourself and others quite differently. It may be an experience of having persisted in carrying out a worthy task when everything within you and everyone around you made you want to give it up. Whatever shape they take, and whatever the immediate or discernible effects, such particular experiences can have a lasting effect on the whole of one's life, an effect that shapes the fundamental style of one's moral life, particularly in times of moral crisis. And, as Edward Robinson points out,

> any system of moral education that ignores this inner, and often quite secret, process of self-discovery ... will be superficial in its appeal and limited in its effectiveness. In the last resort, it will not work. In times of personal crisis the appeal to decency will not be enough.[4]

Such experiences come at various times in people's lives and cannot be keyed to any particular stages. Nor do such experiences necessarily result in "stage-transitions." They are, nonetheless, very important for who we are as moral beings. They often provide the foundation for our own particular kind of moral progress.

A second thing that a developmental approach to moral growth tends to hide is the lapses, vacillations, and even prolonged regressions that are common to our moral striving. Moral development theory sees moral growth as a matter of moving progressively and irreversibly through a hierarchy of stages. But we do not experience the moral life this way. We have moments of clear vision and corresponding appropriate action. But, following on these, we then also experience times of great moral darkness in which we can neither see what is going on nor have any strength to respond. The quality of our moral lives does not necessarily improve in a linear progressive fashion. We have moral reverses, and what is later is not always better. Morally, we can become more egocentric, despairing, and defensive, more insulated from and distrustful of other people, more shallow and less discerning than we were at earlier times in our lives. There may also be times when we come alive again, or for the first time. A developmental theory tends either to ignore such experiences or to explain them away. What we need is an account of moral growth that takes such significant experiences into full consideration.

Finally, a developmental approach to moral life finds it difficult

Moral development —
up-ward, progressive move.

difficulty to attend

to pay attention to the differences between people in their journeys toward moral maturity. By focusing entirely on what is universal in *assumption* morality and on the one psychological structure that is supposed to be fundamental to all moral growth, the developmental approach reduces the immense variety evident in particular individuals' moral journeys to secondary considerations. A look at the lives of saints and other moral exemplars, however, shows them all to be different people who became who they were by quite different paths. If we pay attention to this, we can find much help for ourselves on the highways, byways, detours, and straight and narrow paths that they have taken. If we reduce what happened to and in them to a series of stages that all morally mature people go through, we lose them and, hence, any real understanding of what moral progress involves and amounts to.

Developmental theory sets out a path in advance and implies that all persons who are growing morally are following that path. Developmental theory knows where that path begins and where it ends. To grow morally is to get on track and stay there until the end is reached and growth stops. Charles Taylor puts it this way:

> Genetic psychology operates with two major ranges of basic theoretical notions, those which touch on the nature of maturity—the *terminus ad quem* of development—and those which define innate structures—the *terminus a quo*. The study is, as it were, suspended between these two ranges which determine both its strategy of research and the interpretations it makes of the transformations which the child's intelligence, behavior, and feelings undergo, including, of course, the definition of the stages of growth.[5]

This approach would be fine, of course, if mature morality were in fact able to be fully defined by the *terminus ad quem* (the highest stage), and if moral growth were simply the continuous transformation of one psychological structure (the *terminus a quo*) toward that end. But we have seen that this is not true.

Mature morality is not fully defined by Kohlberg's Stage 6. In fact, mature morality is not even definable. "Maturity" is one of those concepts, like "the Good," that we use to point to a reality that transcends us and recedes into mystery because of its inexhaustible richness. We cannot get "mature morality" defined in any conventional way because, each time we do, we find we have captured too little with the word. Real instances of moral maturity turn out to be more complex and concrete than our definition can handle. If we want to know what moral maturity is like, we will have to look not to general definitions but to morally mature persons. And if we want to know what progressing to moral maturity involves, we will have to pay very close attention to the details of the lives of those persons rather than to abstractly defined stages. When we do, we will find a great deal of variety—all of it illuminating. We will find that there is no one path, no one beginning point, and certainly no one end point. Indeed, we will find that there is no end point at all since moral progress involves the continuously more realistic discernment of and response to an infinitely inexhaustible reality.

The reason the developmental account of moral growth misses these features of our moral journeys is that it tries to do too much and cannot. What developmental studies provide us are accounts of the development of certain capacities. Piaget, Selman, Kohlberg, and others have all rightly discerned and investigated a variety of human capacities that are important for the moral life, and many of these seem to follow a stagelike pattern as they emerge. But moral growth per se is not developmental. The presence of capacities does not determine the quality of one's moral life any more than it determines the quality of one's intellectual life. That quality depends on the use to which those capacities are put, the way in which they are "activated" in concrete, historical circumstances. The absence of certain physical, cognitive, or affective capacities will, of course, put limits on what one can do and be. But the mere presence of a capacity is no guarantee that it will be used in any particular situation, or that if it is used it will be used rightly and well.

When developmental psychologists claim that moral growth is developmental, what they are tacitly, and illegitimately, claiming is that moral growth takes place when certain capacities are available to us. But this is not the case. Moral growth takes place when our capacities are brought to bear in particular experiences and patterns of experience. And this is what, as moral philosophers and moral educators, we need to be concerned with.

Indeed, the study of the development of natural human capacities, fascinating and important as it is, may not be so critical for education as we sometimes think. The reason for this is that such developments tend to occur in most people rather naturally and automatically no matter what sort of educational program is put forward. One of the defining characteristics of a natural developmental stage is that it "be commonly in evidence among members of the species from birth to maturity."[6] What developmental stages define (when they are truly natural developmental stages[7]) are the capacities we have in common as human beings who have lived through common human experiences long enough for all these basic capacities to emerge. Although it is important to know what capacities persons typically have at various points in their lives, an understanding of these capacities cannot provide a full account of what moral growth involves and cannot tell what we need to do in order to guide moral growth in particular and, perhaps, uncommon ways.

I believe, therefore, that in the use of "development" we have settled for an unhappy metaphor. We need to work out other metaphors that will help us to think more comprehensively about changes that take place in the moral life. I have used "growth" and "progress" as my substitutes, but I am not entirely happy with these either. They do not have some of the connotations that development does, but growth may imply too much of an unfolding of what is already there and progress may connote straightforward movement toward a goal. Perhaps we, as Christian educators, would be better off using words that connected our concern here with more traditional and biblical understandings, such as "pilgrimage," "formation," or even "sanctification." In the end, however, it may be best not to choose just one, but to use several in order to indicate the multiple aspects of what we are after, hoping that, as a result, we will all better be able to see our moral journeys in greater fullness and complexity. In the remainder of this chapter and in the next, I want to take a look at several dimensions of moral growth that are left out of the juridical-developmental account, but are especially significant in a Christian understanding of the moral journey.

I have suggested that visional ethics is a mystery-encountering ethic rather than a problem-solving ethic. It is important, therefore, for us to see by what process we come to encounter mysteries.

Michael Foster, in his book *Mystery and Philosophy,* writes: "Christians are called to be holy, and holiness is a mysterious quality; hence Christian ethics is founded on mystery. We have no clue how holiness could be obtained, and are dependent on revelation to show the way."[8] I want to follow Foster's lead here and suggest that one of the crucial experiences we have in the moral life is the experience of revelation, and that through revelation we do encounter mysteries. I want to go on to suggest in addition that revelation is an experience of the transformation of the imagination, and that our character—our fundamental way of seeing and living—changes when this transformation takes place. In other words, I hope to indicate how revelation is important for moral change and can lead to moral growth by describing how the dynamics of revelation are connected to the most fundamental dimension of human selfhood, the imagination. The best way to do this is to begin with a story.

"Revelation"

The story is one by Flannery O'Connor, entitled "Revelation."[9] Mrs. Ruby Turpin and her husband, Claud, entered a doctor's waiting room. They were there to have Claud's leg repaired. He had been kicked by a cow. Mrs. Turpin was a very large woman who seemed both to fill up every space she entered and to order it immediately with bright black eyes that sized up every situation. The room was already crowded by an older woman whom Mrs. Turpin knew to be "white-trashy"; by her ill-kempt five- or six-year-old whose nose ran; by a rather stylish, pleasant woman who wore red and grey suede shoes that matched her dress; and by the stylish lady's daughter, a fat, pimpled nineteen- or twenty-year-old who scowled and read a thick blue book entitled *Human Development.* A younger woman, a redhead whom Mrs. Turpin considered "not white-trash, just common," read magazines and chewed gum. A fat lady who had been seated when they arrived lumbered off shortly thereafter when the nurse called her into the examining room. The radio in the background played gospel music.

Mrs. Turpin could not get comfortable in a place until she knew, by her own inspection, who was who and where they all fit into the scheme of things.

Sometimes at night when she couldn't go to sleep, Mrs. Turpin would occupy herself with the question of who she would have chosen to be if she couldn't have been herself. If Jesus had said to her before he made her, "There's only two places available for you. You can either be a nigger or white-trash," what would she have said? "Please, Jesus, please," she would have said, "just let me wait until there's another place available," and he would have said, "No, you have to go right now and I have only those two places so make up your mind." She would have wiggled and squirmed and begged and pleaded but it would have been no use and finally she would have said, "All right, make me a nigger then—but that don't mean a trashy one." And he would have made her a neat clean respectable Negro woman, herself but black.

She built a scale in her mind of the classes of people. Most colored people were at the bottom—all but the kind she would have been. White trash were next to them—"not above, just away from." The next step up was occupied by homeowners, and above them home-and-land-owners like the Turpins themselves. The scale stretched still higher when it came to people who owned a lot more things than they did and had more money. But here it all became too complicated. Some people who should have been below her had more money, and some people who had good blood and should have had money had somehow lost theirs and were now poor.

As the group sat waiting for their turns with the doctor, Mrs. Turpin and the pleasant lady carried on a conversation that ranged from the condition of Claud's leg to the clock on the wall, the weather, and the care of hogs and nigger help. Mrs. Turpin's hogs were clean hogs: "They're cleaner than some children I've seen. Their feet never touch the ground. We have a pig-parlor—that's where you raise them on concrete . . . and Claud scoots them down with the hose every afternoon and washes off the floor." In Mrs. Turpin's view, nigger help do not do much, and you have to coax them and cheer them and encourage them all along the way. " 'I tell you,' she said and laughed merrily, 'I sure am tire of buttering up niggers, but you got to love em if you want em to work for you.' "

The white-trashy women mutters contempt at all of this, saying, "One thang I know. . . . Two thangs I ain't going to do: love no niggers or scoot down no hog with no hose." At this Mrs. Turpin and the pleasant lady exchanged a look that "indicated they both understood you had to have certain things before you could know certain things."

All the time this conversation was going on, Mrs. Turpin sensed that she was the object of the acute and scornful inspection of the ugly teenager's penetrating eyes. Each time Mrs. Turpin looked at her, she had a stronger sense that this look came from some mysterious region and that it was meant precisely for her. At one point,

> the raw-complexioned girl snapped her teeth together. Her lower lip turned downwards and inside out, revealing the pale pink inside of her mouth. After a second it rolled back up. It was the ugliest face Mrs. Turpin had ever seen anyone make and for a moment she was certain that the girl had made it at her. She was looking at her as if she had known and disliked her all her life—all of Mrs. Turpin's life, it seemed too, not just all the girl's life.

Mrs. Turpin was a thankful woman. Her philosophy of life was to help anybody who needed it, no matter who they were. She was grateful that she could do this and feel this way. Indeed, the thing in life she was most grateful for was her own goodness. She even imagined that if Jesus had given her a choice between being an attractive society woman or a good woman who might be poor or fat or ugly, she would certainly have chosen to be good. As it turned out, he had made her just who she was. She didn't have much, but she did have a little bit of everything and she was good. For all this she was overjoyed with gratitude.

The girl's name was Mary Grace. She went to Wellesley College where she did nothing but study. Her mother thought Mary Grace worked too much. She wanted her to get out and have fun. Mary Grace's mother thought the worst thing in the world was an ungrateful person. She remarked, in Mary Grace's presence, that she knew a girl who had everything a child could possibly ask for, but gave no indication of appreciation. She had nothing kind to say to anyone, and spent the whole of her life criticizing and complaining. To this, Mrs. Turpin had a personal response: " 'If it's one thing I am,' Mrs. Turpin said with feeling, 'it's grateful. When I think who all I could have been besides myself and what all I got, a little of everything, and a good disposition besides, I just feel like shouting, "Thank you, Jesus, for making everything the way it is!" It could have been different!' "

That was when it hit her. The book. It struck her just over one eye, and before she could respond the girl came crashing over on top of her with her fingers clawing into Mrs. Turpin's neck. The world turned upside down and out of focus. Her own insides, a moment ago so full with thanksgiving, went hollow. The doctor and nurse came running, and the others tried to help. But before they could:

The girl's eyes stopped rolling and focused on her. They seemed a much lighter blue than before, as if a door that had been tightly closed behind them was now open to admit light and air.

Mrs. Turpin's head cleared and her power of motion returned. She leaned forward until she was looking directly into the fierce brilliant eyes. There was no doubt in her mind that the girl did know her, knew her in some intense and personal way, beyond time and place and condition. "What you got to say to me?" she asked hoarsely and held her breath, waiting, as for a revelation.

The girl raised her head. Her gaze locked with Mrs. Turpin's. "Go back to hell where you came from, you old wart hog," she whispered. Her voice was low but clear. Her eyes burned for a moment as if she saw with pleasure that her message had struck its target.

Mrs. Turpin sank back in her chair.

When a syringe had brought the girl under control and an ambulance had come to take her away, the Turpins went home. Mrs. Turpin felt dead inside, and could do nothing but lie still on her bed.

The instant she was flat on her back, the image of a razor-back hog with warts on its face and horns coming out behind its ears snorted into her head. She moaned, a low quiet moan.

"I am not," she said tearfully, "a wart hog. From hell." But the denial had no force. The girl's eyes and her words, even the tone of her voice, low but clear, directed only to her, brooked no repudiation. She had been singled out for the message, though there was trash in the room to whom it might justly have been applied. The full force of this fact struck her only now. There was a woman who was neglecting her own child but she had been overlooked. The message had been given to Ruby Turpin, a respectable, hard-working, church-going woman. The tears dried. Her eyes began to burn instead with wrath.

She defended herself in her own mind, but the reasonableness of her claims could not overcome her conviction of having been named. When she told her niggers, their reassurances rang in her ears like lies.

After they had all left and she was alone, Ruby went to the hog-parlor to have it out and find her answer.

"What do you send me a message like that for?" she said in a low fierce voice, barely above a whisper but with the force of a shout in its concentrated fury. "How am I a hog and me both? How am I saved and from hell too?"

"Why me?" she rumbled. "It's no trash around here, black or white, that I haven't given to. And break my back to the bone everyday working. And do for the church."

She dared God to make her trash or a nigger, and threatened to act like one if he didn't. Then came the final assault:

"Go on," she yelled, "call me a hog! Call me a hog again. From hell. Call me a wart hog from hell. Put that bottom rail on top. There'll still be a top and bottom."

A garbled echo returned to her.

A final surge of fury shook her and she roared, "Who do you think you are?"

The color of everything, field and crimson sky, burned for a moment with a transparent intensity. The question carried over the pasture and across the highway and the cotton field and returned to her clearly like an answer from beyond the wood.

Mrs. Turpin stood still. She gazed out at the highway, and then for a long time into the pen of hogs. The sun was setting, and the sky was marked only by a long purple streak. As she looked in its direction, she saw in a way she had never seen before.

She saw the streak as a vast swinging bridge extending upward from the earth through a field of living fire. Upon it a vast horde of souls were rumbling toward heaven. There were whole companies of white-trash, clean for the first time in their whole lives, and bands of black niggers in white robes, and battalions of freaks and lunatics shouting and clapping and leaping like frogs. And bringing up the end of the procession was a tribe of people whom she recognized at once as those who, like herself and Claud, had always had a little of everything and the God-given wit to use it right. She leaned forward to observe them closer. They were marching behind the others with great dignity, accountable as they had always been for good order and common sense and respectable behavior. They alone were on key. Yet she could see by their shocked and altered faces that even their virtues were being burned away. She lowered her hands and gripped the rail of the hog pen, her eyes small but fixed unblinkingly on what lay ahead. In a moment the vision faded but she remained where she was, immobile.

At length she got down and turned off the faucet and made her slow way on the darkening path to the house. In the woods around her the invisible cricket choruses had struck up, but what she heard were the voices of the souls climbing upward into the starry field and shouting hallelujah.

Moral Transformation and the Imagination

Mrs. Turpin makes progress in her moral life in this story. It is not the kind of progress that might show up as stage movement, but it is still a movement toward greater moral maturity. What happens to her is that the shape of her imagination is transformed. The transformation is effected by a "revelation." The result of this transformation is an ability to see herself and everything around her in quite different terms.

Iris Murdoch has said that "in the moral life the enemy is the fat relentless ego."[10] Mrs. Turpin is fat, not just physically fat, but morally and spiritually fat. Her egocentric ordering of people into a hierarchy in relation to herself operates with stunning rapidity. She is able to put everyone in his or her place, and everyone around her seems to sense that this has been done before they have much chance to exist as particular persons for her at all. She achieves this task primarily by putting into operation the conventional images of her own subculture: "nigger," "white trash," "common," "stylish." But she does not just adopt and apply these images from a source extraneous to herself; these images are a deep part of her character and personality. Her dreams and daydreams are full of them, and they form her perceptions and her evaluations of every person and every action. They shine through in her speech and in her gestures. They shape all her own actions and responses.

She is unaware of most of this, and that is what makes her vision so relentless. Her gratitude for her own goodness and her pleasure with her own virtues show how overcome she is with her own vision of the world. Everything is absorbed into it. Her clean hogs, her well-treated "nigger" help, her "doing for the church," her hard work, are all mirrors in which her own goodness and the solidity of her place in her world are reflected. One senses that almost nothing can penetrate her way of seeing, almost nothing can get to her without being first sucked into the powerful mechanism of her distorting ego—nothing except, of course, Mary Grace.

Mrs. Turpin is in many ways a bizarre person. Not many people live in so closed a world governed by so limited an imagination. Still, we know her. We know her because O'Connor displays her to us by inviting us into the subterranean passageways of her consciousness where we see images and forces that work deep inside ourselves. We know when we see Ruby Turpin that we too are symbolic creatures and that our lives are governed by the images that dwell in us. H. Richard Niebuhr has written that

> we are far more image-making and image-using creatures than we usually think ourselves to be and, further,. . . our processes of perception and conception, of organizing and understanding the signs that come to us in our dialogue with the circumambient world, are guided and formed by images in our minds.[11]

This psychic process shapes our world and our character, and provides the foundation for all our seeing, believing, feeling, and action. It is the process we call the imagination.

The imagination is that process in the human psyche which makes meaningful intercourse with the world possible. The imagination is the foundation of ordinary perception, of understanding and interpretation, and of whatever deep probings we may make into the significance, meaning, and mystery of human life and reality. It is not just a cognitive phenomenon, although it is the foundation of all cognition. The imagination is an integrating process that provides the link in the individual between the body, the mind, and the emotions. Mary Warnock, in her comprehensive study *Imagination,* characterizes the imagination as

> a power in the human mind which is at work in our everyday perception of the world, and is also at work in our thoughts about what is absent; which enables us to see the world, whether present or absent as significant, and also to present this vision to others, for them to share or reject. And this power, though it gives us "thought-imbued" perception (it "keeps thought alive in the perception"), is not only intellectual. Its impetus comes from the emotions as

much as from the reason, from the heart as much as from the head.[12]

The imagination's possibility and potency are rooted in images. An image is "an internalized, essentially private, pattern of symbols, pictures, sounds, and sensations of all varieties."[13] As human beings, we are bombarded constantly by sensations of light, touch, smell, sound, and taste. But these do not come to us nakedly. We receive them as beings who sense our own internal bodily movements in relation to them, and as beings who respond to these stimuli in the light of our memories, expectations, and affections. The work of the imagination is to compose all of these external and internal stimuli into meaningful and apprehensible wholes—in sum, into images.

Our very consciousness rests on an unceasing flow of such images, which are constantly being related to one another in particular moments and over extended periods of time. The configurations of images that constitute the shape of each person's imagination determine what we can and do see, think, and feel, and, hence, how we act. The process, of course, is a dynamic one. The fundamental configurations of our imaginations shift and reform in the light of new experience.[14] But the changes are not usually radical, and the more rigid the imagination the more difficult it is for new experience to be experienced as new. Often new experience is not absorbed by the imagination at all (hence, our blindness); or it is absorbed in such a distorted fashion that what is experienced bears no resemblance to reality.

The imagination, then, is an ongoing psychic process that founds human consciousness. It is not a sporadic faculty that can be switched on and off. But it may be used in different ways. On the one hand, we may use the imagination to build up walls around ourselves by imaginatively confining others to conventionally or neurotically defined social roles, thus constructing "a fantasy world of our own into which we try to draw things from the outside, not grasping their reality and independence, making them into dream objects of our own."[15] On the other hand, our imaginations may be used, not to protect ourselves from reality, but to reach out to it. As Niebuhr asserts, "The question which is relevant for the life of the self among selves is not whether personal images should be employed but only what personal images are right and adequate and which are evil imaginations of the heart."[16] Some patterns of imagination lead to a realistic seeing of what is going on within us and before us and, hence, to a real meeting with the world. Others lead to delusion and eventually to the destruction of self, others, and community.

Mrs. Turpin is a captive of an evil imagination of the heart. So long as she remains in this condition, moral progress for her is impossible. Her imagination absorbs everything into her own self, and she has no leverage from within by which to be moved. Whatever natural "development" may take place, she will continue to move within the orbit of her own corrupted imagination. Something from the outside must break the veil of deceit that has over many years come to be built up in her. In order for her to make any progress, her imagination has to be transformed. And, since her imagination runs to the roots of her consciousness, we may say that Ruby Turpin needs to be transformed. The transformation of the moral life, the transformation of character, is a transformation of the imagination.

Imagination and Revelation

A transformation of Mrs. Turpin's imagination does, in fact, take place. When Mary Grace's book hits Mrs. Turpin square in the head and that child comes leaping at her like an avenger from both past and future simultaneously, Mrs. Turpin's entire pattern of vision is thrown into disorientation.[17] But it is not being hit that brings about the transformation. The transformation comes from the message and the sense that it is meant solely for her, lucidly communicated from the depths of mystery. The message is not abstract. She is not told, "You are not a good woman, Ruby Turpin." A message like that could be resisted or absorbed. Instead, the message was a new image, one that could not be absorbed without a revolution of the whole pattern of all her other images, and yet could not be denied, it was so direct. She was "an old wart hog. From hell."

Being a wart hog from hell was not something Mrs. Turpin could have imagined by herself. Such an image had no place in the pattern of her psyche. It had to come from the outside. But when it did come, it had to be taken in. This meant that her whole imagination had to be reconstructed around this new image. She fought it. She struggled with it. She ached to deny it. It was an unreasonable, incomprehensible image: "How am I a hog and me both? How am I saved and from hell too?" But, no matter how paradoxical, she knew it was true and that her own self had to be transformed in order to accommodate it.

The transformation of her imagination was not something that Mrs. Turpin could either carry out by her own power, will for herself, or reason to a conclusion. At this point, her only task was to live with the image and wait. This she did, gazing off at the highway, then deeply into the pen of hogs, and finally across the purple streak in the sky. There she saw the new contours of her transformed self and a new world disclosed. She was no longer at the center of the moral universe. She was simply one reality among many; the same, yet now seen differently. What mattered now was not her place in the social system, for all were marching together toward heaven and all were rejoicing. Even her own goodness, to which she had clung so dearly almost as a weapon, was to be burned away. She had been stripped of an evil imagination of the heart, and had received a new and purer one.

O'Connor wishes us to see what happened to Mrs. Turpin as a revelation. This is appropriate. Revelation and the imagination are deeply connected. In *The Meaning of Revelation,* Niebuhr defines revelation as

> that special occasion which provides us with an image by means of which all the occasions of personal and common life become intelligible. . . . Through it a pattern of dramatic unity becomes apparent with the aid of which the heart can understand what has happened, is happening and will happen to selves in their community.[18]

The function of revelation is to provide us with images by which to see truthfully and realistically. Revelation is not impersonal, however. Nothing is revealed when the images remain objects, part of an external cultural heritage. Revelation is the conversion of the imagination and takes place only when the revelatory images become ingrained in the psyche and provide the framework for all our seeing and living.

Revelatory moments do not live in themselves. They transform and cast light. Their significance lies in the transformation and insight. They provide a new point of view out of which to interpret all that has happened in the past and all that will happen in the future. Such images need to be tested in our ongoing daily lives, and their implications must be worked out through the hard labor of living differently. We do not know what happens to Mrs. Turpin after her revelation. If she goes on to live as before, we will be certain that the vision has failed her or that she has denied its truth and packed it off into some repressed corner of her personality. But she cannot let it shape her and still place herself at the center of the world. She cannot shout "hallelujah" with all the souls on earth and still treat others condescendingly. Revelation must work itself out in the world.

As revelation does work itself out, it will not do so in a way that is unintelligible or irrational. Adequate images are images that help us to see more deeply and clearly into the world; they do not hide it from us or distort it. While the image itself may be bizarre or even paradoxical, the light it sheds is a light that illuminates thought and carries it forward. As Niebuhr says, revelation "brings rationality and wholeness into the confused joys and sorrows of personal existence and allows us to discern order in the brawl of communal histories."[19] But the rationality of the imagination is not always the logic of deduction. Because revelation illuminates selves and history, its rationality will be of a kind appropriate to selves and history: a dramatic or narrative rationality. Revelation will help us to see connections between persons, events, evaluations, and descriptions that we had not been able to see before, because our evil imaginations (sometimes in the guise of a rationalistic, impersonal objectivity) hid them from us.

In this way, revelation opens us to mystery. The tightly controlled world in which we live is exploded by revelation so that the details and depths that were previously hidden from us are now present to us. We are exposed to a wondrous world, which we are drawn to explore. And the more we explore, the more we find being unfolded to us; we never exhaust it. Through revelatory images, a world of inexhaustible particularity, richness, and depth is illuminated. In this experience, we become conscious of having encountered both the mystery of the world and the mystery of the Power in which that world is held and by which our seeing has been made possible.

The Dynamics of Imaginal Transformation

The transformation that takes place in Mrs. Turpin is rather stunning and sudden. I believe that this sometimes really happens to people and do not wish to gainsay that. But for most of us most of the time, the transformation of the imagination is a slow, ongoing process that has few sudden and radical shifts. Does Mrs. Turpin's experience have anything in common with our own less dramatic movements?

I believe it does. Students of the imagination have been able to isolate a pattern that creative imaginal thinking seems to follow.[20] This pattern is found in brief compass in our story, but it goes on over and over again in us as our imaginations undergo transformation. Harold Rugg describes the full act of creative human response as consisting of two basic movements, each with a different orientation.[21] The first movement is the movement of *discovery,* in which the orientation is governed by a groping and intuitive mood. This is partly conscious and partly unconscious, involving the senses, the emotions, and an almost somatic engagement in the struggle to know clearly and rightly. This first movement ends in an illumination and a sense of knowing what one was searching for. The second movement is the movement of *verification.* Here the orientation is one of analysis and interpretation. What one has discovered is now explored, explained, connected with other things one knows, and communicated in various ways to others and tested in the public domain. Juridical ethics seems to put the premium on the latter movement and to ignore the former. But the dynamics of moral vision require that we pay attention to the first as well.

There are three stages in the movement of discovery.[22] First, there is a period, sometimes quite extended, of conscious struggle with a conflict. It is not necessary that one know at this point exactly what the conflict is.[23] Indeed, that may become clear only when the struggle is over. What is necessary is that one sense that something is wrong, that it must be resolved, and that one will not be satisfied until somehow it is.

The conflict may be precipitated by something that happens in the world and to which one must respond. Your company is denying civil rights to women, and you sense you must do something about this. Your nation is involved in a war that you consider unjust, and you must act. All the kinds of public and social conflicts that juridical ethics emphasizes are true conflicts with which we are called to deal. But there are other sorts of moral conflicts as well. They may be internal conflicts concerning our own feelings about someone or something. We cannot help disliking a particular person, but we feel tense and unsettled about this. We feel unhappy with the kind of life we seem to be leading, but do not know how to go about changing that in the least. Or our internal conflicts may have to do with the kinds of descriptive evaluations we are making concerning what is going on in the world, and we sense that somehow these just do not fit—though we are not sure why.

Whatever the type of conflict, creative moral transformation begins in conflict. If such conflicts are briefly felt and then dismissed or repressed, the possibility for movement and growth is aborted. When conflicts arise—either externally or internally—they must be engaged. They are our occasions for moral transformation, our spurs to moral growth.[24]

I b

The second stage in the movement of discovery is an interlude in the struggle. The interlude may take a variety of forms: turning one's attention to something else, falling asleep and dreaming, collapse into exhaustion when the struggle has taken its toll, or a conscious, intentional decision to be expectantly passive and receptive. Whatever the form, there comes a time when conscious struggle has gone as far as it can and the conflict must be given up to other resources.

The function of the interlude is always to loosen the grip of conscious cognitive operations on the conflict. If new patterns of seeing and feeling are to be allowed to emerge, old patterns that have coalesced in consciousness have to be relaxed. So one lets go of the conflict for a time and waits for something to happen. One allows energies and inner resources over which one has no conscious control to do their work, perhaps through dreaming, free association, or off-conscious bisociation of ideas, images, or symbols that are not yet consciously related. Whatever the psychological mechanics, the interlude is an absolutely essential moment in human transformation. William F. Lynch, in his *Images of Hope,* says:

> The decision to wait is one of the great human acts. It includes, surely, the acceptance of darkness, sometimes its defiance. It includes enlarging one's perspective beyond a present moment, without quite seeing the reason for doing so. Fortitude and endurance are there, to an extent, beyond the merely rational. Waiting is sometimes an absolute, which chooses to wait without seeing a reason for waiting. It does not ignobly accept such pseudo-reasons as "don't worry," "don't fret," "don't be silly," "listen to better judgment," "a Christian knows there is no reason for stress." It simply chooses to wait, and in so doing it gives the future the only chance it has to emerge. It is, therefore, the most fundamental act, not the least act, of the imagination.[25]

The final stage in the movement of discovery is the emergence of new insight. The waiting is brought to fruition by the discovery of a resolution to the conflict with which one struggled. This discovery is not something that a person wills or consciously does. It is something that happens to one. The discovery bestows itself, even though it does so from within, intrapsychically.

The insight or discovery comes in the form of a new patterning of the imagination. Often this is a pictorial image in the mind, but it may also present itself as a gesture, as a new way of saying something, or in a new pattern of action. Whatever the form of the insight, it is a creative reorganization of the imagination in which all of the elements of the conflict are related in a new gestalt. The result of such a transformation is a new way of living in relation to the conflict. Resources for thought and action that were previously blocked are now set free. We can see the dimensions of the situation in a way that was not possible before. We know how to respond effectively and appropriately. None of this comes about through the addition of new empirical information or a change of feelings or interpretation. No new empirical information is added, and changes of interpretation and/or feeling are the result of, not the cause of, the insight. The insight is a revisioning of what was there before. We respond differently now because we see differently.

James E. Loder, who has studied the workings of the imagination in a theological context, calls the outcome of this process "the restoration of reality consciousness."[26] This restoration is felt internally both as a release of tension and as a joyous congruence of perception, feeling, and understanding. In this sense, it is an internal reshaping of the self. But it also has outward manifestations. Reality consciousness means being in touch with the world in a more adequate, complex, and truthful way so that "new aspects of reality—and new conflicts—can be explored and readily engaged."[27] The world comes alive to one in a new immediacy, and a realistic ground for intimate and responsive relationship to it is established.

Ruby Turpin goes through the process of imaginal transformation. The conflict is brought irremovably to bear when Mary Grace calls her a wart hog from hell. The conflict has been festering in Mrs. Turpin for a long time, however—a fact of which she may have been tacitly aware. She has struggled ferociously for years with the question of where she fits in the ultimate scheme of things. Her dreams, daydreams, and evaluations of others are all part of this struggle. But when Mary Grace presents her with a new image, the conflict must now be borne in a new way. Her struggle now takes on dramatic proportions. She moves through a series of rationalizations, a search for compassion and reassurance, a violent inner struggle with her own self-image in the light of the new paradox, and finally a furious argument with and challenge of God. None of it brings resolution, and she is spent. Only after a period of stillness, of waiting, of gazing off into the distance and into the depths, does resolution come. It comes through her, but as if from outside of her, as a pictorial image that resolves the conflict, sets her free, and restores her to herself and to the world.

Less dramatically, this same process goes on in us. Usually we do not notice it, because the focus of our attention is not on the process itself. Often we sense that we are struggling with something, but we do not step back and observe ourselves struggling. And when resolution comes, it is not the internal image that we focus on, but the world, which by means of the image is now seen differently. What we sense primarily is not our own psychic processes, but their effects: the sense of release, resolution, and clarity that the process breeds. But anyone who has experienced moral conflict of any kind, who has struggled with it and then either intentionally or out of necessity given it up for a time only to be surprised a bit later by a resolution—a new way of seeing and living through the conflict—has experienced this process. These are experiences that have shaped the contours of our character, have transformed the quality and content of our consciousness, and have occasioned a subtle, silent, but still powerful moral growth.

The process does not happen necessarily or automatically, however. The facts that the imagination is constantly operative in all of us and that all of us encounter all kinds of moral conflicts continually do not guarantee that these conflicts will be resolved or that moral growth will take place. There is room for slippage at many points in the process. The most important of these concerns the engagement of conflict. We do not like conflict. Conflict is painful and brings change. Most of us try to avoid both. A kind of courage and trust is required of us if we are to engage the conflicts that beset us and remain in the tension that they bring. We are fearful people for the most part, and we wish to avoid the creative processes of the imagination as much as possible. Therefore, we often remove ourselves physically and socially from conflictual contexts. If we cannot do this, we ignore them, deny them, or interpret them away. The human psyche is very adept at the avoidance of conflict of all kinds. To avoid conflict, however, is to refuse to enter the process and, hence, to limit both our own growth and the enhancement of the life of the world.

Another place where slippage is possible is at the point of the interlude. Rather than releasing our struggles to other sources, we often give up our struggles and turn to new ones. We find it very hard to be still and open. We fill our minds, our time, and our energies with distractions and anesthetics. Or we push toward premature resolutions to conflicts by making use of stereotypical, conformist, conventional, or shorthand solutions. Waiting for something to happen when you do not know what that might be, and when everything about you and within you pleads for a speedy conclusion, takes some nerve.

Finally, images may emerge that do not really resolve the conflict. It is possible for "false" insights to be bestowed. In this case, what one first thought to be a breakthrough turns out not to have been. The conflict is not really resolved and the tension is not released, even though some sort of insight seemed to have appeared.

> The principle is that if the release fails to appear, then it is evident that the conscious conflict was not the one resolved by the emergent image; an unconscious influence (a conflict concealed from the subject) has entered disruptively into the pattern of reality consciousness.[28]

In this case, it becomes necessary to undergo the process all over again in the light of the recognition that a different conflict is also, and perhaps preeminently, disrupting one's ability to achieve resolution. It is possible, too, that by doing this one may find out what the "false" insight was all about.

Although the insights that arise from the workings of the imagination are personal, spontaneous, and often quite novel, they do not emerge from selves in isolation. Part of what we struggle with when we are engaged in moral struggle are the images that come to us from outside ourselves. One of the reasons adequate images for the resolution of particular conflicts may not appear is that we do not have a sufficiently adequate or extensive repertoire of images to bring to bear. Images are not just intrapsychic phenomena. They are also cultural, available to us in the symbolic systems of our social environments. Revelation is not just the images that emerge from each of us individually at this point in history. Revelation is given, has been given, over a period of history and is there for us to appropriate. Our culture is filled with inadequate symbolic systems, constellations of images that fail us and blind us. But, as H. Richard Niebuhr says, "There is an image neither evil nor inadequate which enables the heart to understand and the event through which that image is given them Christians call their revelation."[29]

Two points stand out. First, if our imaginations are really to bring us in closer touch with reality, they must be informed by adequate and truthful images. Second, Christians believe that what is revealed in their book and in their history provides adequate and truthful images. They have to be reappropriated in each Christian's life, of course, and they have to be brought to bear in new ways through the complex processes of the active imaginations of contemporary individuals. But the metaphors, stories, and images of the Christian faith are symbolic constructions that have come into being by resolving conflicts in the past, conflicts that are perennial and basic to human existence. In the context of appropriate contemporary conflicts, they are available to do their work again. The process of creative imaginal resolution of moral conflict can thus be impeded by an inadequate fund of images at one's command, or aided by a symbolic universe that provides images that really do help us to see reality.

The process is often short-circuited, but not always. When it is not, we grow morally and achieve a more adequate vision of the world. This is a never-ending process, however. There are people who can do what we have described more adequately than others, and this is what makes them moral geniuses. But even for them, there is no highest stage or end point for growth. Reality is always greater and deeper than our experience of it. The moral conflicts that make us grow never cease.

Conclusion

The process of moral growth through the transformation of the imagination is not the only way we make moral progress, but it is one very basic and important one. It makes its impact at the fundamental level of our consciousness and character by shaping and reshaping the ways in which we see the world and understand ourselves. The imagination is foundational to all of our seeing, believing, feeling, and acting; and any shift of its contours is also a transformation of ourselves as moral beings.

Experiences that we have of resolving moral conflict by means of imaginal transformation are quite often exactly those experiences that give our lives their particular shape and quality, and out of which our responses to life often seem to flow. In such experiences, the deepest patterns of the nature of reality and existence, and of our relationship to them, are revealed, and our own essential convictions are rooted in them.

In addition to giving us a past and a place out of which to live, however, these experiences also give us a way of living in the future—a way that promises to keep changing us throughout our lives. By living into and through the conflicts that meet us, we learn to trust and even welcome circumstances and contexts in which the process may be gone through again. Though the process may be painful, the restoration of self and world that it brings is profoundly satisfying and serves as an impetus for further growth.

Though the process is satisfying, we are not always able to sustain it. For many reasons, we may be blocked in our striving to grow morally in this way. When this happens, we often experience dry periods of moral stagnation or even regression. Moral growth does take place through this process, but it is neither automatic nor irreversible. Though the dynamics of the imagination are fundamental to human development, moral growth through imaginal transformation is not itself developmental in the sense that one moves progressively through higher stages. Each person's journey is a particular and unique journey, the course of which is not marked out in advance.

4
Disciplines: Repentance, Prayer, and Service

moral growth comes from process of dis-valuing ego-centric views.

Moral growth involves the increasing apprehension of mystery.
This takes place when we no longer put ourselves at the center of the
universe, succumbing to the illusion of moral egocentrism. To move
out of the center requires a transformation of our imaginations. The
evil imaginations of our hearts must be purified and reformed. This
is accomplished, sometimes in sudden and striking ways and more
often in prolonged and more subtle ways, through revelation.

The transformation of our imaginations through revelation is *Introduction*
not something we can accomplish by our own powers alone or
achieve by force of will. It is a gift that is given to us. It is an effect of
grace. But this does not mean we have no responsibility for our own
moral growth. Only if we are willing to receive can we do so. And, as
Diogenes Allen points out, "we have to change in quite specific ways
to get into the condition which allows us to perceive mysteries."[1]
Getting into that condition requires that we undertake certain disciplines.

The importance of discipline in the moral life has become
obscured in our culture and in the church as well. The stress on
autonomy in the moral life has led to an emphasis on the independent powers of the individual, which we are afraid might be stifled or
restricted by too much training or dependence on the guidance of
others. Creativity in morals and almost everything else results, we
think, from allowing what is inside a person to be freely expressed.
And true expression depends more on leaving people alone than on
helping them to be molded through the disciplines of the "school
figures."

disciple def.

But Christians have historically understood the formation of the moral life as formation in discipleship. To be a disciple is to be an adherent of the way of Christ. It is to be a follower of his, and to have one's life formed through the strenuous discipline of going where he went, looking at things the way he did, trusting as he trusted, making ourselves vulnerable as he was vulnerable. If we believe that reality is revealed to us through the eyes of Christ and that our lives are transformed by being with him, then the way to grow morally is to undertake the discipline of becoming disciples.

There are, I am sure, many ways to describe the disciplines of the Christian life. Each different way will highlight some aspects and ignore others. But there are three disciplines that seem to me to be fundamental and generic. They are the disciplines of repentance, prayer, and service. Through these disciplines, the church has trained its people for discipleship—for active engagement in the world as persons formed by Christian faith. I believe these disciplines merit our renewed attention if we are to be effective Christian educators for the moral life.

Repentance

I suggested earlier that one of the differences between juridical ethics and visional ethics is that the former does not take sinfulness very seriously while the latter does. There is a corollary to this. Juridical ethics finds no place for the discipline of repentance. For visional ethics repentance is utterly essential.

2. If our problem is really sin—a fundamental breach in human existence—then repentance, not self-improvement, is the first requirement. This is the biblical view of the foundations of morality. The prophets, John the Baptist, Jesus, and Paul all beckoned their hearers to a new life by calling them first to give up the old in repentance (Mark 1:15; Luke 13:3, 5; Acts 26:20; Romans 2:4; II Corinthians 7:9–10). Repentance is the absolutely inescapable first step of the Christian moral life. Without repentance, the Christian moral life is impossible.

Repentance is often thought of in terms of being sorry for, and asking forgiveness for, particular transgressions. This, admittedly, is often the biblical context for the mention of the idea. But, if this were all there is to it, repentance would be perfectly compatible with the concept of the self-sufficiency of the independent reasonable person. After all, even reasonable people make mistakes, and it is appropriate for them to admit them. But Jesus and Paul regarded sinfulness and the need for repentance as something much deeper. For them, sinfulness was a profound alienation from God, and, therefore, from reality. In our sinfulness, we do not know reality as mystery. It is reduced to a mere object and distorted in fantasy. So we cannot be related to the world as it is.

Repentance, in the New Testament, refers to a reorientation of the whole self. We have talked of sin as our striving to establish and sustain ourselves by our own power against the threats to our existence and security. Repentance is a *metanoia*, a turning from the self to God as the source of our establishment and sustenance. As such, it is a recognition of one's sinfulness, of one's utter incapacity to make oneself good and whole by one's own powers, and of one's utter dependency on God and constant need for grace. The reorientation is thus a displacement of our own self-establishment and self-sustenance from the focal point of our psychic and physical energy. It is a "letting go" of all that, leaving it in the hands of Another.

But repentance is not only a reorientation. It is also a transformation of the self. As Jean Calvin puts it, "Departing from ourselves, we turn to God, and having taken off our former mind, we put on a new."[3] This transformation involves a sacrifice, a kind of death:

> Therefore, my brothers, I implore you by God's mercy to offer your very selves to him: a living sacrifice, dedicated and fit for his acceptance, the worship offered by mind and heart. Adapt yourselves no longer to the pattern of this present world, but let your minds be remade and your whole nature thus transformed. Then you will be able to discern the will of God, and to know what is good, acceptable, and perfect. (Romans 12:1–2; NEB)

We are called, in repentance, not only to turn in a new direction, but to allow a great change to take place in ourselves. This is perhaps the most frightening and difficult thing about repentance. We are not being called to *make* a great change in ourselves; that would be hard,

fear of losing one-self

but at least we could maintain control over it. We are to give up control and allow something to happen within ourselves that we cannot foresee. We are to give up "the pattern of this present world," which tells us who we are, what is expected of us, what the rewards and punishments will be of acting and thinking in certain ways, and let ourselves be remade from top to bottom. The great fear in all of this, of course, is that we will lose ourselves—that we will disappear.

Repentance, if it is this kind of turning and openness to transformation, requires two things: humility and trust. Repentance requires the humility involved in the confession that I am a sinner, one whose life is not whole and who lacks the power both to find either the direction to wholeness or the resources for wholeness on my own. Repentance requires trust in a power that can and will ultimately sustain and establish me if I let go of myself into that power's hands. Without both trust and humility, repentance is impossible.

But, as Donald Evans makes clear in considerable detail in his book *Struggle and Fulfillment,* trust and humility come only as the fruit of struggle. Trust is a struggle against anxiety, wariness, idolatry, despair, and apathy, which "is personally experienced as a disorderly daily scrimmage between forces which usually do not identify themselves until there is a temporary truce and the dust of battle has settled for a while."[4] Humility is a realistic acceptance of both my actual powers and my actual limitations. It is a struggle against both pride ("a self-deceptive attempt to act out my infantile fantasies of infinitude, of unlimited strength and status"[5]) and self-humiliation ("a self-deceptive attempt to ignore my real though modest powers and achievements, preferring instead to wallow helplessly in shame"[6]).

These struggles, as Evans and, before him, Erik Erikson show, are struggles that begin in our earliest years and continue in different ways throughout our lives. Repentance is something we are not capable of until trust and humility have to some degree become characteristic of our lives. We must be able to bring ourselves to repentance in humility and trust. But in repentance, our trust and humility are tested, refined, and deepened. The trust and humility that I have make it possible for me to offer myself to God—trust and mistrust, humility, pride, self-humiliation, and all. And what I find then, according to the promise of the Gospel and the witness of the church, is that my trust is grounded in the trustworthiness of God and that my humility has its basis in God's acceptance of me. I offer myself, risking the possibility that my trust will be shattered and my self-acceptance found unacceptable. I find instead that I am given myself back again as a gift. I find myself established and sustained by One who has established and sustained me before and through my struggles, and who can be depended on to establish and sustain me for all time.

The fruit of repentance is the availability to me of the mystery of myself, the world, and God. The availability to me of the mystery of myself allows me to be free with respect to myself and to tap depths within myself that are beyond my direct control. In the freedom to be myself that repentance brings, I can let go of willful control of myself and be receptive to what lies deep within me. Evans puts it this way:

> A man allows himself to be changed by an upsurge of vital energies which impel him in unforeseen directions. When a man is open to the inner dynamism of the psyche he loses the security of the order which he has already imposed on his life. If he empties his mind of the orderly structures which he has concocted as his defense against inner chaos, and waits expectantly for something to happen, he somehow overcomes his anxiety, somehow trusts the forces within him in spite of the risk. The new freedom which then may come is a spontaneous, creative freedom.[7]

If, in repentance, I give up self-establishment and self-sustenance, I also become more free to see others as they are because I am less captive to the need to distort them for my own purposes. I am free to perceive and accept the world as it is and to give myself to it without fearing that I will lose myself in doing so. Here we see most clearly the vital connection between repentance and morality. Repentance is becoming unself-conscious in a way that allows me to become receptive to the world. The persistent need of the unrepentant ego to establish and sustain itself builds up indestructible walls between ourselves and the world, making it impossible to relate in appropriate and responsible ways without selfish distortion. But when the diabolical process of fattening the ego is given up in repentance, we are able to accept and respect the inexhaustible particularity of others and to shape our attitudes and actions to their fundamental needs.

Finally, repentance makes the activity of God available to me. Repentance is not making; it is allowing. Repentance allows me to be receptive to myself. It allows me to be met and shaped by others as they really are. It also allows God to work God's transforming craft in me. To quote Evans again:

> God cannot act in a man unless the man permits it. Instead of being receptive to divine activity a man can block, impede, and resist it. Instead of allowing God to liberate him, a man can reinforce his own self-imprisoning defenses. God does not help those who help themselves; he helps those who realize their own need of help. God creates new life in those who acknowledge the destructive elements in their lives and let go of them. God speaks to those who are willing to listen to him. God is present to those who are open to receive him.[8]

So repentance is a "letting go," in trust and humility, of our striving to control everything in order to establish and sustain ourselves. It is a turning to God to allow God to meet our needs in a way that makes possible a transformation of ourselves.

Repentance is a crucial movement in the Christian moral life and one that is never completed. It is a continuing discipline that we undertake at increasingly deeper levels, bringing more and more of ourselves to God in humility and trust. We repent by bringing our ideas, our desires, our offenses and offendedness, our plans and goals, our values and convictions as living sacrifices to be taken from us and returned to us, transformed and made new. Saints never cease repenting, but repent more and more deeply as they increasingly recognize the depth and breadth of their dependence on God and of the mystery of the world.

Prayer

Prayer & repentance are related

Repentance and prayer are deeply related. We need to pray for our repentance, and repentance makes possible better prayer. The two build on and nourish each other. But there is a sense in which prayer follows on repentance. We must see this in order to understand what prayer is and how it shapes us morally. In repentance, we let go of ourselves in order that we may be receptive to God and to the mysteries of reality. Through repentance God's power becomes available to work in us. Prayer moves us further. More than receptivity to God, it is attention to God. Repentance is the discipline of opening ourselves. Prayer is the discipline of paying attention to *God*, what, by our repentance, God gives to us.

I have learned to think of prayer as attention primarily from two persons: Simone Weil and Brother Lawrence. Weil says that "prayer consists of attention. It is the orientation of all the attention of which the soul is capable toward God."[9] Brother Lawrence considered prayer to be "the practice of the presence of God," and described his discipline as one of trying at all times "to keep myself always in God's holy presence by simple attentiveness and loving gaze upon Him."[10]

If this idea that prayer consists of attention to God seems strange to us, perhaps it is because we have given up the discipline and no longer really know how to pray. In most of our praying, our attention is neither focused nor on God. What we attend to is largely our own selves, and this in a rather generalized and ambiguous way. Prayer, both public and private, and particularly among Protestants, tends to be almost totally prayer of petition. We have some need, and we pray that it will be met. We are in some trouble, and we pray that God will take it away. Even when we do pray prayers of praise, thanksgiving, and confession, we do so with our attention turned to what we are pleased with, thankful for, and guilty of. We find it extremely difficult to allow our praise, thanks, confession, petition, and intercession to be formed by attention to God, and awfully easy to allow the God to whom we pray to become a mere reflection of our own concerns. At least this is what I experience myself as a prayer and what I perceive in most public worship. "Simple attentiveness" is most difficult. It is also very important.

Prayer as attention to God

Prayer shapes us morally. Murdoch tells us, "The religious believer, especially if his God is conceived of as a person, is in the fortunate position of being able to focus his thought upon something which is a source of energy."[11] The reason religious believers are fortunate is that attention to sources of energy that are good provides the power and direction to move away from evil. If we are involved in a destructive relationship with someone, if we are addicted to a way of living that is making it impossible to live fully, if we are at war with ourselves and with others, it does little good to tell ourselves to stop. "What is needed," says Murdoch, "is a reorientation which will provide an energy of a different kind, from a different source."[12] What we require "is the acquiring of new objects of attention and thus of new energies as a result of refocusing."[13] When we become absorbed in something else, the original object of our attention no longer has its pull on us. We are almost automatically obedient to what absorbs our attention.[14] This is why prayer is the necessary discipline for obedience to God.

Prayer, or attention to God, is the most difficult form of attention. We have not seen God, and it is very hard to pay attention to what we have not seen. Furthermore, we are compulsive idolators, and our attention to God is easily diverted to attention to idols. We do not start, then, in the discipline of prayer, with attention to God. That is our goal. We start by learning to pay attention to what God has given us, the reality before us. Such attention is practice in prayer. It is also an implicit form of prayer. To really attend to and love the natural world, art, ideas, and other people is indirectly to attend to and love God.

Jesus shows how this is so by telling the parable of the sheep and the goats (Matthew 25:31–46). Those who receive the Lord's blessing are those who, in the course of their lives, are able to pay attention to the hungry, the thirsty, the stranger, the ill, and the imprisoned. It turns out that, unwittingly, they had all along been attending to God in Christ. Prayer, in its implicit form, is the act of attention to realities that are before us. By such acts, we attend, indirectly, to God. Through such acts, God's very self is made known to us, and we are thus more able to pray explicitly.

One of the more manageable places we can begin to learn to pay attention when we are starting in the discipline of prayer is in trying to learn something new. Weil suggests that "school exercises" can be "extremely effective in increasing the power of attention that will be available at the time of prayer."[15] In order for such learning to be effective for our attention, however, we must want to learn solely for the sake of knowing the reality. If our purpose is to increase our skill, look accomplished in the sight of others, get rewards, and so forth, we will not learn how to pay attention; we will only learn how to use things for other purposes. This means that learning something involves trying to do it correctly and refusing to ignore our errors.

Paying attention in our studies, Weil says, is not to be confused

with a kind of muscular effort. If one says to one's pupils: "Now you must pay attention," one sees them contracting their brows, holding their breath, stiffening their muscles. If after two minutes they are asked what they have been paying attention to, they cannot reply. They have been concentrating on nothing. They have not been paying attention. They have been contracting their muscles.[16]

Attention is quite different: "Attention consists of suspending our thought, leaving it detached, empty, and ready to be penetrated by the object; it means holding in our minds, within reach of this thought, but on a lower level and not in contact with it, the diverse knowledge we have acquired which we are forced to make use of."[17] Paying attention means holding back our preconceptions and our desires for how things should be until the object of our attention has had a chance to make an impact on us. Thus, the first step of attention is closely related to repentance. Attention in school studies requires a kind of intellectual repentance that lets go of the tendency to think we know all about something before we have really studied it at all. But attention goes further. It allows the reality before us to move us and change us. Once the object of our attention is seen, we allow it to change our preconceptions if necessary and to reaffirm what truth we previously knew. Attention takes us out of ourselves, and then changes us to bring us more in accord with reality. When this happens we are thankful and joyous—both for the reality we have come to know and for our relationship to it.

Attention to human beings is more difficult than attention in school studies. Human beings are much more complicated, threatening, and hard to understand. But the process is much the same. To love persons is to attend to them just as they are. In attention to persons, "the soul empties itself of all its own contents in order to receive into itself the being it is looking at, just as he is, in all his truth."[18] This means withholding conventional labels, refusing to compare the other's status or prestige with my own, allowing the other to accept or reject what I have to give, refraining from manipulating the other into meeting my needs, granting the other his or her separateness and independence from me. All of this is very hard to do, and is possible only if we are free to do it because our own needs are met by God. But doing it is something we can learn by discipline.

As we practice these disciplines, we come closer to prayer itself. But prayer as attention to God is not the occasion for the disappearance of attention to the world. Attention to God purifies our attention to the world and provides the energy and light we need in order to do it. Murdoch says that there is a place for "an attention which is not just the planning of particular good actions but an attempt to look right away from the self towards a distant transcendent perfection, a source of uncontaminated energy, a source of new and quite undreamt virtue."[19] Attention to God in prayer requires that we turn our attention from the world for a time. But this, as Murdoch goes on to say, "may be the thing that helps most when difficulties seem insoluble, and especially when feelings of guilt keep attracting the gaze back towards the self."[20]

Service

The theme of service is a prominent one in the Bible, and particularly in the Gospels. Several times the Gospels report that the disciples argued about who would be nearest to Jesus in the coming Kingdom. In response to these arguments, and in other situations, Jesus always made it perfectly clear that those who would be near him, those who would follow him and be his disciples, would be servants.[21] Likewise, we who would undertake the disciplines of discipleship must undertake the discipline of service.

One of the most powerful images of service in the Bible is Jesus washing the feet of his disciples (John 13:1–17). At our seminary, we have chapel services every Tuesday and Thursday morning. The text for one of these days happened to be John 13, and the worship leader planned not only to preach on that text but also to have us celebrate the "sacrament" of foot-washing. But through a typographical error, perhaps inspired, the announcement went out that we were to have a "fool-washing." The slip seemed right. The brightest and the best, the powerful and authoritative in our world, do not wash people's feet; only fools do. To become a servant is to undertake a foolish discipline.

The foolishness of service is not immediately obvious. After all, our society is full of volunteer service groups and professional social service agencies. These are widely recognized to be involved in good and important work that it is wise and laudatory to support and to accomplish. Helping others is a well-respected activity. There are, however, different ways of helping others. The discipline of service, as that is presented to us in the Gospels, is a distinctive way of helping others, one that, by the world's standards, seems foolish. Simone Weil expresses the difference this way:

> It is not surprising that a man who has bread should give a piece to someone who is starving. What is surprising is that he should be capable of doing so with so different a gesture from that with which we buy an object. Almsgiving when it is not supernatural is like a sort of purchase. It buys the sufferer.[22]

The Christian idea of service is distinctive in that it buys nothing. It is a "good for nothing" kind of service. It is service that is obedient simply to the fact of a person in need who requires our attention whether what we have to give will ameliorate that person's need or not.

In our culture, service is tied intimately to effectiveness.[23] That is, we do not consider a service to have been rendered to someone unless that service changes that person's condition in a material way. We have not served the ill unless we cure their illness. We have not served the weak unless we make them strong. We have not served the lonely unless they are no longer lonely. We have not served social outcasts unless we make them socially acceptable. Now I am not suggesting here that it is necessarily better to remain ill, weak, lonely, or socially outcast. Nor am I suggesting that we should not help people toward health, strength, and fellowship with others. But I do want to point out that, where our sole aim is effectiveness, certain diabolical dynamics are set in motion.

Effectiveness requires power and the use of power. And if we are to be effective, the power must be in our hands. Power and the use of power are not in themselves evil. But the gathering of power into our own hands in order to be effective regularly turns into the gathering of power in order that we may be and remain powerful. When this takes place, we are no longer servants; we are masters. We find ourselves no longer obedient to the needs of others; we are obedient instead to the demand of maintaining and exercising power.

This has an undercutting effect on the ones whom we initially wish to serve. For, if service is linked too closely with effectiveness, we become the ones who must decide what effectiveness means. In taking power into our own hands in order to be effective, we must determine what the one in need will become when our service is accomplished. We become the definers of health and strength and fellowship, and thereby deny the ones in need of their freedom and personhood in illness, weakness, and loneliness. Rather than servants, we become manipulators. Service becomes self-serving. We say, in effect, "You will most fully exist for me when you have become—through my service to you—what my power enables you to become." When this happens, the one in need has become ours. We have bought the sufferer.

In addition to these problems, effectiveness as a criterion of service is unrealistic. There are, in fact, many situations in which what we wish to do for another simply cannot be done. Effectiveness requires too high a view of our own power, and too high a view of ourselves in relation to those whom we wish effectively to serve. In practice, we find this out. When we do, this knowledge can become an occasion for distance between ourselves and a sufferer. If service must be effective, then when we can no longer be effective we no longer have any reason to be there with and for the sufferer. The sufferer, by becoming an occasion for our effective use of power, becomes an object with which we can dispense when our power is seen to be ineffective.

The idea of service as the effective use of power is paradoxical at its center. Effectiveness requires the accumulation of power; but to be a servant involves a renunciation of power. This is why the discipline of service in the Gospels seems so foolish. It says there is a way of helping others by renouncing rather than by accumulating power. There is a service whose criterion is not effectiveness, but something else.

At the heart of service lies, not effectiveness, but *presence.* Service as presence means being *with* another. Christ's service to humankind was not effective in the sense that he brought an end to suffering and death, to illness, loneliness, weakness, social isolation, confusion, or political turmoil. Christ's service was his incarnation— his coming to be with us to take on our sufferings as his own, to stand with us and to go through with us whatever it is we are going through. When Jesus commanded the disciples to wash one another's feet saying, "I have given you an example that you also should do as I have done to you" (John 13:15), he was commanding them to be present to others as he was present to them.

Simone Weil seems to have understood what this meant. Indeed, she took it so seriously that it became an obstacle to her being baptized and joining the church. In a letter to a dear friend of hers, a priest who wished her to enter the church and who was instructing her in what that would mean, she wrote that she was afraid that entering the church would mean separating herself from the multitude of unbelievers. She said:

> I have the essential need, and I think I can say the vocation, to move among men of every class and complexion, mixing with them and sharing their life and outlook ... merging into the crowd and disappearing among them, so that they show themselves as they are, putting off all disguises with me. It is because I long to know them just as they are. For if I do not love them as they are, it will not be

they whom I love, and my love will be unreal. I do not speak of helping them, because as far as that goes I am unfortunately quite incapable of doing anything as yet.[24]

Weil practiced that vocation. Though she was a philosopher and university teacher, she abandoned that work to be employed for a long period of time in a Renault factory in France. She went incognito. Her service was not to teach or improve, but just to be with people and to experience what they experienced.

Presence is a service of vulnerability. To be present to others is to put oneself in the position of being vulnerable to what they are vulnerable to, and of being vulnerable to them. It means being willing to suffer what the other suffers, and to go with the sufferer in his or her own suffering. This is different from trying to become the sufferer. Presence does not involve taking another's place. That would be demeaning. It would suggest, "I can take your suffering better than you can, so move aside; I will replace you." Instead, presence involves exposing oneself to what the sufferer is exposed to, and being with the other in that vulnerability.

The words "equality" and "justice" take on their most important meaning in this context. Presence demands equality and justice in the sense that it renounces the self-protection of power over the other and of whatever power could be summoned against the threats the sufferer endures. We do have power over others and power against threats to ourselves. Some people are stronger than other people: physically, intellectually, emotionally, socially, politically. Justice means refusing to use that power in order to avoid for oneself the position that another is condemned to. We are not born equal. Justice makes us equal. Service, presence, is not possible without it.

The sign of presence is compassion. When we are truly present to another our passions are linked. This is different from pity and even from empathy. Compassion is not feeling sorry for another. Nor is it just feeling inwardly in a way that corresponds to what the other feels. Our passions are the way we embody our life energies. In passion, what moves in us and through us shows in our faces, movements, and gestures. Compassion is allowing the life of another to move through me, to *move* me, so that I reveal, bodily, the impact of the other's life on me.

Vulnerability and justice make compassion possible. But compassion itself is the greatest service. When we are suffering, our deepest need is not the alleviation of our suffering but the knowledge that our suffering does not annihilate us. We know that we have not been overcome when we see our own life energies register in the face of another.

Mother Teresa of Calcutta is for many an exemplar of the life of Christian service. Her work is not noted for its effectiveness but for its compassion. She saves few lives, but those who are picked up out of the street starving and dying receive new life. It comes to them through her face. It is radiant. And they are aware that her radiance comes from seeing them.

Finally, presence involves commitment. There are moments of particular vulnerability when equality makes compassion arise in especially striking ways. But such moments do not take place unless time has had its chance with us. We need to be with others over the long haul. Compassion demands that presence will not quit with the moment. It implies a future in which presence promises to be maintained. This is perhaps the feature of service that most makes it a discipline. Vulnerability for just a moment is not really vulnerability at all. Equality that threatens to turn quickly into inequality when the threats become too great is bogus. In order to serve, we must become servants and not just provide services.

Service, then, is a discipline of renouncing power in order to be present with others in vulnerability, equality, and compassion. Ironically, such service does help people. It is, in a kind of foolish way, effective. It repeatedly has the effect of providing space for other persons to tap their own resources and to gather their own energies. It also provides opportunity for a person in need to feed off of the powers of the servant. Here the one served draws power, freely and not under coercion. The one served is recognized as the person he or she is, and is not made into an object. The service of presence provides nourishment for body and spirit; it does not manipulate the flesh.

Those who have grieved over the death of a loved one know how this is true. The people who are most help to us in this situation are not the ones who try to do something for us. They are instead ones who suffer with us. They allow themselves to be vulnerable to what has happened to us and refuse to deny either the death or its pain. They do not place themselves at a distance from us but make themselves equals. They are the ones whose compassion expresses itself in the way they look at us and hold us. In them we see a natural reflection of our own selves, and not a forced pity. The sight of their faces illuminates our darkness and gives us a sense of life.

The experience of the service of others is one we have in a variety of circumstances, however—not just when we suffer. Not only in our suffering, but also in our joy are we blessed by people who can be with us there. We can be, and need to be, served by others in whatever we are going through. If, for example, we are trying to learn something new, the teacher who serves us is one who goes with us in learning. We have all had the unhappy experience of being taught by someone who we sensed was too soon where we are expected to end up. This teacher pushes us, pulls us, and does everything else in his power to make us get where he knows we ought to be. But if we are fortunate, we have also been taught by another kind of teacher who we sense knows the way but is willing to wait and see what happens on the journey this time. Everything is not all decided in advance, and what happens in my learning will make a difference to her. She is willing to become my equal and to be vulnerable to what takes place. I see in her face that my own learning moves her, and that she is committed to me and my learning over the long haul. We recognize such teachers to be the ones who have really served us. They are the ones who brings us and our learning to life.

3   The discipline of service is a discipline through which care, concern, and aid are given by one person to another in a particular way, in a way that is shaped by presence—vulnerable, just, compassionate, and committed.[25] This discipline is integrally related to the disciplines of repentance and prayer. Just as prayer presupposes repentance but also deepens and refines it, so, too, does service presuppose, deepen, and refine repentance and prayer.

Service depends on a letting go of our self-protectiveness. The drive to establish and sustain ourselves is the main deterrent to vulnerability. To be both self-protective and vulnerable is a contradiction; they cannot both be maintained. Furthermore, the very dynamics of self-establishment and self-sustenance build up walls of injustice and inequality between people. We fatten our egos precisely by putting ourselves above and at a distance from others.

Likewise, service depends on prayer in both its explicit and implicit forms. We must be able to see people as they are, we must pay attention to them no matter their condition, before we can be in a position to be with them. And compassion and commitment require not only attention to another, but also the kind of energy that flows through us when our own life forces are purified by attention to God.

But service also affects the quality and degree of our repentance and prayer. In service, we recognize the limits of our own power and are made humble. In the experience of service, we realize more profoundly than in any other that all lives, not just our own, are established and sustained by a Power that lies outside of any of us. Through service our attention is drawn increasingly to that Power, and we find ourselves learning to pray in new and more obedient ways.

Worship as Paradigm

These three are the fundamental disciplines by which the moral lives of Christians grow. They are disciplines of discipleship, and through them we move more and more into a position where the mysteries of reality can be revealed to us. As we repent, pray, and serve, we ourselves are less and less central to our concern. We put ourselves out of the way so that God can do God's work in us. We get ourselves into a condition in which our imaginations may be transformed so that we can come to see, think, feel, value, and act as reformed selves.

Christians have a paradigm by which these disciplines are made known to us and acted out symbolically. That paradigm is worship. In worship our disciplines take on liturgical form, but they are the same disciplines nonetheless. When we come to worship, we come to put ourselves in a position to receive revelation. Worship is repentance, prayer, and service carried out in the context of a hearing of God's Word.

Our orders of worship reflect these disciplines. When we are called to worship, we are reminded of the presence of God and our attention is drawn to God. We come as repentant people, and our prayers of confession are our attempts to recognize ourselves as sinners in need and as ones who would turn from ourselves toward God. We come to pray to attend to God by singing hymns and saying prayers of praise, thanksgiving, intercession, and petition. We pray in a different form as we pay attention to God's Word in scripture, in preaching, and in the sacraments. And we do not come alone. We come with others who are there with us as equals and whose status or condition in the world is of no consequence. We are present with one another in God's presence, and present to one another as we receive each other in baptism and share with one another at Christ's table.

Of course, in worship we live through these disciplines symbolically, and the patterns of our living may not live up to the patterns of our liturgy. But worship is not "mere" symbol or ritual. These symbolic actions have a way of training us and shaping us at preconscious levels so that over time their order becomes imbedded in us. In worship, we see and sense who it is we are to be and how it is we are to move in order to become. Worship is an enactment of the core dynamics of the Christian life. This is why worship is its central and focusing activity. It is paradigmatic for all the rest of the Christian life.

The activity of worship is mandatory for those who would have their moral lives formed after the pattern of discipleship. In the ritual of worship we learn how the whole of our lives is to be shaped. To grow morally means, for Christians, to have one's whole life increasingly be conformed to the pattern of worship. To grow morally means to turn one's life into worship.

The Disciplines in the Life Cycle

From the way I have described the disciplines of the Christian moral life, it should be obvious that undertaking them in their fullness is an adult activity. These are not disciplines that children are capable of undertaking *as disciplines,* consciously and intentionally. Children are, however, capable of repentance, prayer, and service *as acts,* usually spontaneous and sporadic. I believe that repentance, prayer, and service are significant throughout the human life cycle, and that their relevance is not confined to adults. I want to show how this is so.

In order to do this, it is important first to make the connection between the disciplines and the dynamics of imaginal transformation discussed in the previous chapter. The connection is this: The disciplines are ways in which we intentionally put ourselves in particularly fundamental situations of conflict, engage them, and then wait in order to allow something to happen in us.

The discipline of repentance engages us in the fundamental conflict over the foundations of our existence. To discover the source of our establishment and sustenance we must struggle. Unless we make this struggle, we do not enter into the discipline. But the discovery depends on an interlude, a "letting go." It is only in this letting go that the discovery of the source of our establishment and sustenance is made. In the same way, it is a struggle to pay attention—to God or to anything else. As Weil says, "Attention is an effort, the greatest of all efforts perhaps, but it is a negative effort."[26] It is the negative effort of putting away distraction, of refusing to allow other things within us or outside us to displace the object of our attention. But a kind of waiting is required here, too. Attention requires a relaxation that allows us to be penetrated by what we attend to. Our work is in holding ourselves open; attention then comes of its own. Conflict is also involved in service. By becoming vulnerable we open ourselves to powerful forces, and it is a struggle to remain there. Commitment means staying in for the long haul, and that, too, is conflict-laden. But once we are there, we must pause to wait. Only then does compassion flow. It cannot be forced. It must be allowed to come.

The disciplines, then, are particular ways in which we intentionally move ourselves into the process by which our imaginations are transformed. But, as we saw with Ruby Turpin, it is sometimes possible for us to be thrown into the process. In some such circumstances we may find ourselves repenting, praying, and even serving in spite of ourselves. This, I think, often happens with children—especially quite young ones.

In order for repentance, prayer, and service to take place as acts, all that is required developmentally is the capacity to imagine. This capacity becomes available very early in life. Indeed, as Erikson has shown, the imagination has its roots in the interplay between a mother and an infant. By the third month, infants have the visual capacity to see their mothers' faces. As they are fed and held and cared for, they watch that face as it "shines upon" them. Through the interplay between mother and child that goes on here, the mother "lets herself be verified as the first comprehensible image."[27] This image and the process by which it came to be, says Erikson, provide the rudimentary pattern by which the imagination develops. It also makes it possible for the infant to engage the first central conflict of human life, the felt "dread of being alone in a universe."[28] The coming and going of that face makes the infant aware simultaneously of a universe and of its fragility.

Conflicts keep coming throughout our lives, and the task of the imagination is to deal with them. As our imaginations develop, the conflicts become more complex, differentiated, and conscious. The watershed in this development comes with the emergence of what Piaget calls "the symbolic function." This marks the arrival of the capacity to evoke, by means of symbols, objects that are not actually present.[29] In other words, the child now has the capacity to form mental images that can be evoked at will. This capacity, which emerges at about one and one-half to two years, is preconceptual and prelinguistic. But just this capacity is required for engaging in the creative process. Now the child can use symbols to form a world that does not depend upon what is happening at the moment. Conflicts can be lived through over time and resolved.

Sometimes children resolve the conflicts they have by making the movements of repentance, prayer, and service in a rudimentary way. Edward Robinson has related an experience reported to him that I think illustrates this.

When I was about five I had the experience on which, in a sense, my life has been based. It has always remained real and true for me. Sitting in the garden one day I suddenly became conscious of a colony of ants in the grass, running rapidly and purposefully about their business. Pausing to watch them, I studied the form of their activity, wondering how much of their own pattern they were able to see for themselves. All at once I knew that I was so large that, to them, I was invisible—except, perhaps as a shadow over their lives. I was gigantic, huge—able at one glance to comprehend, at least to some extent, the work of the whole colony. I had the power to destroy or scatter it, and I was completely outside the sphere of their knowledge and understanding. They were part of the body of the earth. But they knew nothing of the earth except the tiny part of it which was their home.

Turning away from them to my surroundings, I saw there was a tree not far away, and the sun was shining. There were clouds, and blue sky that went on for ever and ever. And suddenly I was tiny—so little and weak and insignificant that it didn't really matter at all whether I existed or not. And yet, tiny and weak and insignificant as I was, my mind was capable of understanding that the limitless world I could see was beyond my comprehension. I could know myself to be a minute part of it all. I could understand my lack of comprehension. . . .

Although my flash of comprehension was thrilling and transforming, I knew even then that in reality it was no more than a tiny glimmer. And yet, because there was a glimmer of understanding, the door of eternity was already open. My own part, however limited it might be, became in that moment a reality and must be included in the whole. In fact, the whole could not be complete without my own particular contribution. I was at the same time so insignificant as to be almost nonexistent and so important that without me the whole could not reach fulfillment.

Every single person was a part of a Body, the purpose of which was as much beyond my comprehension now as I was beyond the comprehension of my ants. I was enchanted. Running indoors, delighted with my discovery, I announced happily "We're all like ants, running about on a giant's tummy!" No one understood, but that was unimportant. I knew what I knew.[30]

This is an experience of repentance because the child reveals both a certainty that she is accepted, valuable, and indispensable in the world (established and sustained), and a realization that she is not at the center of attention of the universe and that this is as it ought to be. These two certainties are the opposite of moral egocentrism; they are the essence of repentance. This is an experience of prayer, because it contains evidence of deep attention to particular beings and a sense of the limitless depths of reality as a whole. In commenting on this report, Robinson himself says:

> The nature of prayer is something about which I find it increasingly hard to speak. We should all however agree that central to the essential attitude of prayer is a kind of opening up of the attention, a turning outward from the immediate concerns of the ego to a wider awareness. . . . And in this capacity . . . the child has the adult beaten at every turn.[31]

There is evidence here, too, of the fundamental dimensions of service. The child recognizes her vulnerability to be equal to the vulnerability of the ants, and she is willing to accept that. She knows she has the power to destroy them, and yet does not do so. She has compassion for them.

To point to instances like this is not to argue that children can be morally mature. I want only to suggest that repentance, prayer, and service are possible at almost every age in the human life cycle. People can grow morally at every stage of human development. Moral growth takes place when whatever capacities we have are activated in repentance, prayer, and service. And, as we have seen, this can happen in some form at all but the earliest ages.

I have argued that moral growth per se is not developmental. But there is a connection between the movements of repentance, prayer, and service and the development of natural human capacities. As we develop, these movements become more complex. Human development opens broader and more complicated worlds to us. The forms that repentance, prayer, and service take will change in the light of this.

For example, the convergence in later adolescence of formal operational thinking (Piaget), the identity crisis (Erikson), and the capacity to organize the perspectives of other persons in a systematic way (Selman) opens up a significantly more complex world to pay attention to than the world of childhood. At adolescence, a more complicated and usually more insecure self must be given in repentance. Finally, the world to be served and the dynamics of service have dimensions to them that were previously hidden. Repentance, prayer, and service, then, become more difficult tasks in adolescence than they were in childhood. The same is true, of course, in different ways in adulthood.

Natural human development on all registers places one in new situations, makes one conscious of hitherto unknown features of human experience, and makes possible increasing ability to communicate with others and to reflect systematically on one's condition. As a result, the range and complexity of moral experience, as well as the existential tensions generated by it, increase with development. This means that the movements of repentance, prayer, and service will themselves be significantly more complex and difficult to make, though perhaps more profoundly and maturely made when they are made.

Not only do the world and the movements become more complex, however. Our relationship to the world also becomes more intentional. As we become more mature developmentally, the movements of repentance, prayer, and service increasingly take on the character of disciplines. Less and less are they spontaneous and sporadic acts. We become more aware of what we are doing and more responsible for the shape of our lives. We come increasingly to choose or refuse to repent, pray, and serve.

The relation between moral growth and natural human development of physical, intellectual, psychological, and social capacities can be summarized, then, as follows: (1) Moral growth can take place within all of the developmental stages by the actualization of repentance, prayer, and service, using whatever capacities one has at that stage. Within each stage there is potential for moral growth or stagnation, depending on the degree to which these movements are made. (2) Natural development has the effect of increasing the range and complexity of moral experience, and, hence, the range and complexity of the movements of repentance, prayer, and service. (3) Development brings with it increasing intentionality in and responsibility for these movements. They, therefore, increasingly take on the character of disciplines. (4) The fact that development takes place does not guarantee that repentance, prayer, and service will. Development does not ensure moral growth. At all stages of human development, moral egocentrism, lack of attention, and failure to serve are possible.

From Loved One to Stranger

The disciplines of the moral life are related not only to human development; they are also related to the contexts in which they are undertaken. We grow morally not only when the movements of repentance, prayer, and service are made in the more complex ways that human development demands. We grow also as we make these movements and undertake these disciplines in a broad variety of contexts. To be receptive, attentive, and of service to those closest to us—our loved ones, friends, and neighbors—is one thing. To do so with enemies and strangers is more difficult. But the moral life does not fully mature unless the latter is done.

We can try to live in a world surrounded by loved ones and friends, closing out others who as enemies threaten us or who as strangers are potential threats. But no matter how receptive, attentive, and serving we may be in such a world, life lived there alone is not morally mature. Until enemies and strangers are encountered in repentance, attention, and service, we simply do not know or have the opportunity to experience the depth at which these movements may be made. Loved ones and friends do not, by definition, present as deep and persistent a threat to our establishment and sustainment as do enemies and, potentially, strangers. Unless, therefore, we encounter these, we have failed to make the movements at a level the term "maturity" connotes.

Furthermore, it is only when we come to face those who seem most alien to us that we are able to face what is most alien in those who are closest. It is often more difficult, for example, to allow ourselves to be vulnerable to and really see a friend's anger than it is to do so with the anger of an enemy. My spouse's loneliness is harder to take than the loneliness of a stranger, and I am more inclined in the first case to refuse to recognize it. The reason for this is simply that, with those closest to us, the threat and alienation strike more centrally into the core of our personhood. In these circumstances, our own selves are more deeply vulnerable. We may have to be receptive, attentive, and of service to strangers and enemies before we are able to be more deeply attentive to the most strange and threatening dimensions of our loved ones and neighbors.[32]

Encountering enemies and strangers is not just a matter of deepening disciplines, however. The moral life involves loving enemies and strangers. We are called to break down those barriers between ourselves and others that make us enemies and strangers. Repentance, attention, and service are initiatives we can take to bring those who were once enemies or strangers to us as friends and loved ones.[33]

The Church and Moral Growth

We grow morally as we repent, pray, and serve in the increasingly complex ways that human development requires and in the variety of contexts that range from relationships with loved ones to strangers. We cannot do this alone, however. We need to be in a community that supports us, guides us, and undertakes these disciplines with us. For Christians that community is the church.

The church is the worshiping community. We are that body of people who are learning together to repent, pray, and serve in the light of our history and an imagination that is teaching us to do so. The focus of our history and imagination is Jesus Christ, in whom we see what it means to live in repentance, prayer, and service. We seek to follow him, to be his disciples, and to undertake the disciplines that such a life requires.

As we follow him, we see that we cannot be the church and remain a closed system of intimate and exclusive social relationships through which we are protected from the world. To the extent that we actually are being transformed in repentance, prayer, and service, we find that we must continually strive to rupture our own boundaries. The church is just not the church except as it seeks to incorporate within its mutuality enemies and strangers. Its repentance, prayer, and service is for all people, for the world as such, and not just for others as Christians.[34] In the church we are impelled by the very dynamics of what it means to be the church to meet the enemies and strangers of our lives.

Most institutions are defined in terms of exclusion and care for their own. The church is not. This is why the church as a repenting, praying, and serving community is so significant for the shaping of the moral life. We can learn the disciplines of the moral life only in communities that provide resources for the breaking of self-securing, both personally and institutionally, and for attention and service to all the world. The church has such resources. These are the resources on which we must draw as we educate for the moral life.

III EDUCATION

5
Moral Education
in the Church

Moral education is not something that we in the church do in addition to Christian education. Christian education is education for the Christian life. Since this life has a moral dimension to it, Christian education has a "for the moral life" dimension, which is neither separate from nor a mere adjunct to Christian education as a whole. We cannot do Christian education without its being moral education. And the moral education of Christians cannot be done in any fullness apart from Christian education.[1]

Themes and Experiences

When we look at the Christian life, we see certain themes as being particularly helpful for articulating and describing its moral dimension. These themes include an understanding of all persons as sinners who have a natural and anxious concern for ourselves, which distorts our perceptions of and relationships to other human beings and to reality as a whole; a recognition that we cannot remedy this condition by our own power, and are in need of a relationship to God, which transforms us; and an acknowledgement that we are required to get ourselves into a position in which this transformation can be worked in us. These themes set the parameters for the church's understanding of the moral life. When the church takes this understanding seriously, it undertakes certain disciplines in response: the disciplines of repentance, prayer, and service. When these disciplines are undertaken, certain experiences result. These experiences are the ones that, through education and other means, the Christian community hopes to pass on, because it believes that these experiences shape us morally. But what are these experiences?

The church, as it repents, prays, and serves, experiences itself as established and sustained by Christ, whom it follows and in whom it lives. Its experience with Christ changes the people in the community. They become what they were not before. They sense that, because Christ has come into their midst and because they are drawn to him and follow him, they have become new persons, received a new life. In Christ, believers see a power at work that turns them from themselves and from the self-destructive patterns of living they had been entrapped by as they fought to establish and sustain themselves by their own power. The center of their psychic and emotional energy shifts from the desire to protect themselves against themselves and others to a freedom and capacity to live for others. As a result, such people become increasingly able to attend to and serve others. They are more open to the needs of others and sense themselves to be newly alive in their ability to respond.

In Christ, self-preoccupation begins to disappear in a way in which it never could without the presence of Christ. As a result, people feel much less burdened, able to think more clearly, and able to do things they could not do before. Christians find that they are living a different life, because they have a new point of reference that brings everything else into focus. They recognize this new life as something they have been given in their experience with Christ, and know that it is not something they have or could have achieved by themselves. Everything they are they owe to what God has done in and for them through Christ. Because of this they continue to follow him and strive to open themselves increasingly to him, so that they may grow in this new life. They continue to repent, pray, and serve; because they know that it is only by deepening receptivity and attention to him as he is known in the scriptures, in the witness of the history of their faith, and in the way their present life is illuminated by him that their new life can continue to be lived.

Those who experience this new life recognize that they experience it in and through their community. The new life is fundamentally and essentially a shared life. The sharing takes at least two forms. It is a sharing of persons in interpersonal mutuality. People participate in one another's lives on a deep level that is increasingly less self-defensive and mutually manipulative. It is also a sharing of the new point of reference that brings the new life. Christians tell to one another the stories of Christ's life, death, and resurrection, and of the experiences that have been reported as these stories have actually changed people's lives. They know that, if these stories are told again, their own experiences and the experiences of others may be deepened in this way of living. They find these experiences difficult to relate without recourse to metaphors and images that point to the nature of the experiences and their source, but do not explain them away or reduce them to what is ordinary and experienced by all.

The impact on the moral life of these experiences is that, in being freed from the burden of establishing and sustaining the self over against others, we are freed to live for others. We are able to see our loved ones in a new light. Because affection, anger, or indifference can no longer ultimately engulf or destroy us, we are free to see our loved ones more as they really are. This enables us to serve them, care for them, bear pain and suffering with them, open ourselves and give ourselves to them, without fearing that in doing so we might be used in such a way that we will be destroyed.

The same is true for our relations to our neighbors or peers. Because we know we are already established and sustained by that which is indestructible, we are no longer under compulsion to hurt others in order to keep from being hurt, or to better others in order to place ourselves above them. We experience freedom to give to our neighbor what the neighbor needs, and to receive from our neighbor precisely what the neighbor has to give.

But this freedom is available not only with respect to those to whom we are naturally close. We are also free to give to and receive from enemies and strangers. The freedom that comes with being established and sustained by God through Christ is a freedom to go out into the world where there are known threats and dangers, and assumed hostilities. People are enemies because they threaten each other. In the new life of the repenting, praying, and serving community, however, we who experience it are decreasingly threatened. This opens up the possibility for breaking the mutually destructive cycle. The enemy is no longer wholly a threat. The stranger, too, is no longer one who, because he or she might be a threat, can be ignored or turned away. The stranger is one who, like all others, is uniquely made, a gift of God. The stranger is, therefore, one who is worthy of being received, attended to, and served just because he or she is there.

To be able to regard others in this way is to be receptive and attentive to them as inexhaustible particulars. As we become increasingly receptive and attentive, we come to see all people as unique mysteries whose depth may be increasingly revealed, but never exhausted. Depth is revealed as people are present to one another. To be present to someone is to be in communication with that person in such a way that we have a deepening sense of who that person is and how that person is related to the perfectly loving and creating source of being who is God. Presence is unself-conscious in the sense that the other absorbs our full attention. But by giving ourselves to others in this way, we simultaneously receive the gift of ourselves. And in being given ourselves, we know how to act with regard to others. Others are no longer problems to figure out. They are mysteries, the very apprehension of whom compels fitting and appropriate action.

The experiences I have described are uncommon, but they are real. They are experiences that the church as a repenting, praying, and serving community has had and continues to have. They are experiences in terms of which Christian believers sense what it really means to be moral. They are experiences that Christians believe are central to moral growth, and that the Christian community must place at the center of its Christian education for the moral life.

Christian education for the moral life, then, is the introduction of persons to and the incorporation of persons within this realm of experience. The introduction of persons to this realm of experience involves describing and showing it to people through an articulation of its dimensions and a retelling of the experience as it has taken place in both historical and contemporary settings. The incorporation of persons within this experience means finding ways to help people have the experience themselves in the context of a concrete, living Christian community.

If we think of moral education in the church in these terms, we can outline what it is in the way shown in Figure 1. The top half of the figure deals with the nature of the experience of the church as a repenting, praying, and serving community. The bottom half deals with the nature of the educative process by which persons are

FIGURE 1

Christian Education for the Moral Life

Is

The Introduction of Persons to
and the Incorporation of Persons within

Established and Sustained by Christ Whom It Follows and in Whom It Lives	The Experience of the Repenting, Praying, and Serving Community	A Context of Interpersonal and Imagistic Mutuality

As It Increasingly
Receives, Attends to, and Serves

Loved Ones, Neighbors,
Enemies and Strangers

And Expresses Itself in
Appropriate Understanding and Fitting Action.

Teachers   and   Learners

Investigate,
Share,
and
Take Responsibility for
This Experience

As They Become Involved in
A Creative Teaching-Learning Process

at

Appropriate Times

in

Appropriate Settings

in

Ways Appropriate to Their Own Capacities

introduced to and incorporated within this experience. The two are related by the fact that the experience of the community becomes one's own experience while one's own experience becomes part of the community's experience as one shares it and takes responsibility for it. The task left before us, then, is to explore in some detail what this approach to moral education in the church means.

Community as Educator

People cannot be introduced to or incorporated within a repenting, praying, and serving community unless there is one. In other words, Christian education for the moral life depends heavily on the mode of living of the Christian community. Education for the moral life takes place in a context, and that context must be one that continually seeks, however imperfectly, to receive, attend to, and serve all persons and institutions on the basis of decreasing need for self-establishment and self-sustenance and, hence, self-defense.

Persons learn the moral life in a context in which they themselves are received, attended to, and served as inexhaustible mysteries, unique from all others and valued as such. They also learn the moral life only as they live in a community where all others are regarded in the same way as well. Therefore, the community must be one in which the boundaries between itself and its environment are broken through.

During the summer of 1967, the strength and height of these barriers became painfully and frighteningly obvious to me. The city of Detroit, like other cities across our nation, was burning in racial riot. I was a teenager then and, lying in bed at night, I could hear the gunfire in the distance as people in the city took to the streets to shoot at one another. I could hear the sirens of police cars and fire trucks. Tanks and jeeps patrolled the streets. Black people were embittered, angry, hot, and at the end of their ropes. White people were scared to death. Many bought guns or loaded the ones they had, and carried them in the back seats of their cars or took them to bed with them to protect themselves and their families. I remember my own fear and confusion.

On the Sunday after the riots, we went to church. We waited to hear the preacher, who had helped us to struggle with issues like this before. What would he say in that congregation filled with white people, many of whom held positions of power in the city? What we heard was the sermon "Seeing the Invisible."[2] The preacher turned our attention to Moses, who "endured as seeing the invisible" (Hebrews 11:27). We, who had been thinking mainly of ourselves, were called to "seek to find out why these riots occur—why people are so frustrated, so outside our society, so hopeless. . . ." We were reminded how only a few could see Jesus after his "stupid, indecent, lawless, and frightening death." And we were told that "a Christian is one who sees the invisible." The preacher said, "We must see not only that which is on the surface, but be able to see Jesus—see what is at the heart of things; that love suffers long and is kind; that love vaunts not itself, is not easily provoked; that love bears all things, believes all things, hopes all things, endures all things." And we were asked: "WHAT IF YOU DO SEE HIM—now invisible in the midst of all that is happening? If we saw Him would we not be filled with shame and discontent living in a kind of self-centered myopia—short-sighted and blind to what endures? If we really saw Him, would we sit down and act as if we had to expect the worst—or that the best was to be taken from us?"

The walls of Jericho did not come tumbling down as a result of that sermon. The city was not transformed and evil has not been overcome. But some members of that congregation saw beyond the paralysis of fear. The New Detroit Committee was born to bring white people and black people together to begin the long, slow, painful process of rebuilding the city. The chair of that committee, and a moving force behind the effort, was a member of the congregation that heard that sermon.

Where it depends for its life on God alone, the church can break through boundaries set up to protect itself from threats to its own insecurities. It can be a community in which strangers and enemies as well as neighbors and loved ones are met, received, attended to, and served. Outside such a context moral education is subject to distortion. Moral education is easily subverted by attempts on the part of communities to fortify their own positions and to use their capacities and talents to increase self-establishment and self-sustenance under the pretense of following moral norms. The church does not and has not, of course, always provided a satisfactory context for moral education. The point is, however, that the church as Christ's body increasingly becomes an open context or ceases to be what it intends to be. Outside such a context as this, moral growth toward maturity is ultimately impossible.

The quality of the social context in which we live either limits the ability of individuals to make moral progress or invites them into ever greater progress. The life of the community as a whole determines the quality of teaching and learning for the moral life that is possible there. A community characterized by self-establishment, self-sustenance, and lack of receptivity, attention, and service to others cannot be a morally educative environment no matter what principles it espouses, what stories it tells, or what claims it makes for itself.

To say all of this is to say little more than what C. Ellis Nelson, John Westerhoff, and others have said concerning the power of the socialization processes of communities for shaping lives.[3] A community shapes our perceptions, values, and identities by the many subtle ways it uses language, sets norms, makes decisions, and carries out actions. All that I am adding to their insights here is a criterion by which the adequacy of a community's socialization processes may be judged. That criterion is the depth of its engagement in the disciplines of the moral life.

The Significance of a Teacher

Though the community as a whole is the essential context for Christian education for the moral life, and though the character of that community determines greatly the kinds of experience we can have there, life in the community is not all there is to moral education. The community provides a context for learning, but teaching is also essential to the educational enterprise. By teaching, I mean the intentional activity of one person that consists of guiding the learning of another. Because teaching is an intentional activity, it cannot mean just the serendipitous influence one person might have over the learning of another. In teaching, the teacher actually hopes for certain changes in another person's life (in knowledge, thought processes, insights, perceptions, feeling, and/or action), and acts in ways that will facilitate those changes. The teacher is a person who is intentionally responsible for involving learners in the experience of the repenting, praying, and serving community in such a way that its various aspects might be explored, shared, understood, and participated in.

The relationship between a teacher and the community is a bit complex. A teacher does not stand apart from the community and its experience to point it out to learners from a distance. A teacher is a part of the context, and the experience is his or her own experience. Therefore, when teachers introduce learners to the community's experience, they, in part, introduce the learners to themselves. Because of this the person and role of the teacher are inextricably intertwined.

To be a moral educator demands that a person be a certain kind of person, and the skills involved in teaching in this domain cannot be had apart from this. The primary and basic act of the teacher must be to be receptive, attentive, and present to the learners. Whether a student is able to learn the disciplines of repentance, prayer, and service depends on the student's experience of being received and attended to as a unique individual valued as such and related to in the mode of presence by a teacher. Such acts on the part of a teacher are not the mere application to the learner of an objective technique. They are not something that one can do without first having undertaken the disciplines oneself. To be a moral teacher, then, one must have had one's character shaped by the disciplines and be able to regard each student in the light of who one has come to be through them. The teacher must be capable of being available as a servant to the learner; and this is only possible to the degree that the teacher is free to refrain from manipulating the student in some way to enhance the teacher's own self-establishing and self-sustaining mechanisms.

This is not simply a matter of modeling for a student a moral way of living. Just having models is not enough. The teacher does not set before the learner a model for him or her to emulate, but rather develops a relationship with the learner in which the learner is freed to respond with receptivity, attention, and service to the receptivity, attention, and service first given to him or her. Education for the moral life can really begin only when the teacher and the learner accept each other as persons. The role of the teacher is to initiate this relationship and provide the grounds for its mutuality.

Martin Buber, in a discussion of the role of the teacher, says:

> There is only one access to the pupil: his confidence. For the adolescent who is frightened and disappointed by an unreliable world, confidence means the liberating insight that there is human truth, the truth of human existence. When the pupil's confidence has been won, his resistance against being educated gives way to a singular happening: he accepts the educator as a person. He feels he may trust this man, that this man is not making a business out of him, but is taking part in his life, accepting him before desiring to influence him. And so he learns to ask.[4]

Only when the learner is apprehended as an inexhaustible mystery, and not as a problem to which the arsenal of the teacher's techniques are to be applied, can Christian education for the moral life take place between a teacher and learner. This involves being present to the learner:

> The teacher must be really there, really facing the child, not merely there in spirit. . . . He need possess none of the perfections which the child may dream he possesses; but he must be really there. In order to be and to remain truly present to the child he must have gathered the child's presence into his own store as one of the bearers of his communion with the world, one of the focuses of his responsibility for the world. Of course he cannot be continually concerned with the child, either in thought or in deed, nor ought he to be. But if he has really gathered the child into his life then that subterranean dialogic, that steady potential presence of one to the other is established and endures. Then there is reality between them, there is mutuality.[5]

On the basis of this mutuality of presence, which is initiated and made possible by the teacher's receptivity and attention, moral education takes place.[6]

The person and role of the teacher are inextricably intertwined in another sense. The teacher is not simply one who is there for the student. The teacher is one who is receptive and attentive to a much wider reality as well. Out of this wider receptivity and attention, the teacher has come to see the world in a particular way. To the extent that the teacher has truly received and attended to this reality, the teacher apprehends some truth and value. The role of the teacher includes directing the attention of the learner to this truth and value. It includes showing the learner around the world. Buber puts the matter this way:

> What we term education, conscious and willed, means a selection by man of the effective world: it means to give decisive effective power to a selection of the world which is concentrated and manifested in the educator.[7]

This is an overwhelming and frightening responsibility. It is a responsibility that most contemporary theories of moral education have attempted to shirk by arguing that what is true and valuable is determined by each of us individually, or by arguing that what is true and valuable is manifested in rational principles that can be clearly and objectively understood apart from the person of anyone who holds them. But we have seen that truth and value are features of the world that are apprehended only by persons who have to some degree pierced through the veil of the distortions brought on by moral egocentricity. Truth and value are revealed to others by just and living persons who in their life and language provide a glass through which to see.

When we are present to one another, we begin to see reality in terms of the descriptions of the way life is seen that these people use. This cannot, and should not, be avoided. But it means that the teacher has authority. This is not an authority the teacher imposes on the learner, but one the learner accepts and responds to because of the fact of their relationship. The teacher, therefore, cannot avoid teaching truth and value as he or she sees it and lives it. The teacher must assume responsibility for this authority, and strive to make sure that the truth and value that is taught, that the effective world that is selected, is truly worthy and good. How worthy and good the truth and value are that the teacher brings the learner to see depends on the person of the teacher as affected by the depth and range of the teacher's own movements of repentance, prayer, and service. Of course, the teacher may abdicate this responsibility. But in so doing, the teacher fractures the bonds of mutuality that provide the grounds for the possibility of moral education in the first place.

In Louisville, a young adult member of a large congregation works with a group of four teenage girls in a way that exemplifies responsible authority in teaching. She gathers the girls into her home weekly for Bible study. They began meeting because the minister of the church felt there should be some group of young people doing Bible study in the church. The teacher responded, somewhat hesitantly, to the minister's request that she lead the group, and the four girls were the only ones who still came after the first few meetings. The teacher was nervous for the first several months. The girls all seemed so different—not ones who would naturally be attracted to each other as a social peer group. The girls seemed to hide from each other and from the teacher for a long time. But as they studied together, they got to know each other better. The biblical texts began to bring questions to the surface they had hardly dared ask before. And they found, in their conversations, that their lives were asking them similar questions.

The teacher, by listening patiently and attentively to these questions and by responding to them out of her convictions and experience, came to know the girls and love them. And the girls have come to know and love her. This fall they have undertaken a study of Mark. They are learning the difference between God and mammon in the Bible and in the local high school. They are exploring what it means for a person to be unclean (Mark 7:20–23). The teacher is helping them to deal with the pressures on them to conform to their peers, with their confusions, fears, and desires in sexual relationships, and with their problems with their parents. Together they explore the scriptures in the light of their concerns and their concerns in the light of the scriptures. Together they are learning to see their lives in new ways. Their teacher is, for them, a trusted guide.

The significance of a teacher is the significance of a particular person who we know cares for us and cares about what we know and see and experience. Such a person is willing to show us around the world and point out to us what is true, valuable, and good. Teachers are concrete incarnations of the experience of the Christian community who are able to mediate and make available to learners the dimensions and depths of that experience. We do not learn from people in general. We learn from particular people who give themselves as a conduit for us into a vision of the community of which they and we together are a part.

Encounters, Images, and Interpretations

The role of the teacher is to be a caring conduit into the experience of the church as a repenting, praying, serving community. This can be done only as the teacher and learners together encounter the loved ones, neighbors, enemies, and strangers of their world in the light of images that help them all to be receptive, attentive, and of service. Moral education in the church is practice in the disciplines of discipleship. Learning these disciplines involves facing the conflicts that encounters with others bring on us. It involves going through a creative process through which these conflicts are resolved: a process that includes struggle informed by the images, stories, metaphors, and histories of the Christian faith; times of waiting that allow the imagination to be transformed; experiences of discovery and resolution that allow us to live through the conflicts in new ways; and enterprises of interpretation in which the struggles and their resolutions are analyzed and communicated. Teachers help learners to learn the disciplines and to appropriate the experience of the community for themselves as they guide them through this process.

In doing so, the teacher's first task is to discover who the loved ones, neighbors, enemies, and strangers of the learners are and what some of their conflicts with them might be. It is not hard to imagine, for example, that many young people will already be struggling with

conflicts with their parents over questions of authority and obedience; with schoolmates over questions of social pressure, cliques, and
alternative life-styles; with girlfriends and boyfriends over the relationship of sex to friendship and love; and with persons of other
races and classes over issues having to do with prejudice, isolation,
and fear. It is not hard to imagine adults struggling with spouses
over the use of money, the distribution of responsibilities in the
household, and the way time is spent together and apart; with
employers and colleagues over questions of competence and competi-
tion; with political figures over the use of power and the distribution
of rights and goods; and with interest groups that threaten their own
life-styles. The teacher must be sensitive to what these struggles are,
and must then make decisions about which to bring up for exploration.

The second step is to provide resources that will help the
learners explore the dimensions of these struggles. Among these will
certainly be biblical resources. Narratives, histories, parables, and
images from the scriptures that may shed some light on the struggles
themselves should be given to the learners to read, ponder, explore,
and discuss. Resources from the history of the church and accounts
of the experiences of other Christians in analogous struggles should
also be used. Studies of biographies and autobiographies can be
especially illuminating. Novels, plays, poetry, music, and other art
forms can also be very helpful.

The point of bringing these resources to the learners in their
struggles is emphatically *not* to provide ready-made answers. The
purpose is to help learners to see and live through their conflicts in
the light of images that they may rework and reorganize, often
unconsciously, in their own creative processes to make discoveries
that will help them to see more clearly what is going on.

The third step in the process is to stimulate actual encounters
between the persons in conflict. If, for example, a youth leader senses
that racism is a controlling distortion in the young people's relationships with others, a series of meetings between the youth and persons
of different races might well be called for. By bringing these people
together, the teacher evokes conflicts already in the young people's
consciousness, brings them to the surface, and sharpens them in such
a way that they can no longer be ignored. In short, the teacher

confronts the learners directly with the conflict in such a way that they are compelled to work it through.

This step will not always take the form of setting up encounters directly. A teacher may develop formats for encounters that take place at the learners' initiative. Students may work with the teacher to develop interview guides, and then go out to interview parents, neighbors, or strangers. The teacher may suggest and facilitate counseling relationships in some cases. The use of field trips into new and somewhat threatening places is often a powerful way to begin helping others to broaden their worlds.

The point in all of this is that the teacher takes the responsibility for providing situations in which actual encounters between learners and their loved ones, neighbors, enemies, and strangers can take place so that the conflicts that are latent may be brought to the surface and dealt with. Encounters with others are not, however, merely occasions for stimulating our own creative processes. They are occasions in which we come to know others and, through interaction with them, come to receive them more fully, see them more realistically, and perhaps be present with them more compassionately. The actual presence of these persons, and not just a distant thinking about them, makes such interactions possible.

The role of the teacher is important here because learners cannot always set up these encounters themselves. This is especially true with regard to enemies and strangers. The teacher may be a friend or loved one of someone who is a stranger or enemy to the learners. The teacher functions as an intermediary who introduces people to each other and makes the encounters possible. Sometimes, it is only through the mediation of a teacher that learners can encounter some strangers and enemies.

The teacher does more than just set up an encounter, however. The teacher also shapes it by raising questions, offering his or her own perspectives on it, encouraging the parties to explore more deeply, and pointing out the possibilities for growth and resolution if they continue in the encounter. What the teacher has to say during and after these encounters is very important for helping learners to explore and to understand what they have explored. Helping learners to find the right words and concepts to use in describing the encounter and in searching more deeply is critical. Words and concepts take on their significance and meaning as they bring new light to what the learner is actually experiencing. Murdoch makes this point in her description of one way in which moral learning takes place:

> Learning takes place when [normative-descriptive] words are used, either aloud or privately, in the contexts of particular acts of attention. . . . As Plato observes at the end of the *Phaedrus,* words themselves do not contain wisdom. Words said to particular individuals at particular times may occasion wisdom. . . . Use of words by persons grouped round a common object is a central and vital human activity.[8]

The teacher's task is to find words, and help others find words, which actually do clarify what is going on.

Martin Luther King, Jr., was a powerful moral teacher because he confronted white people, physically and immediately, with black people and described them to each other as human beings, brothers and sisters, rather than as slaves, misfits, or intractable enemies. These are all normative-descriptive words. The moral teacher teaches by helping learners, in the context of encounters with particular realities, to come to normative-descriptive words that really fit, and that provide a new vision that can help us find a new way through our conflicts.

As much as it is the teacher's responsibility to guide the explorations of the learners, the teacher does not and cannot pretend to do the exploration for the learners. What the teacher sees is important. But it is not so important as that the learners see, and see in their own terms. The revelation of the mystery of a particular reality is not the teacher's to give. Teachers do not provide new ways of seeing, or the appropriate understanding and fitting action that follow from it. Rather, they provide occasions for the learners' own new visions, understandings, and actions. What we hope for, as teachers, are insights, understandings, and actions that arise out of the learners from their own repentance, prayer, and service. Such insights, understandings, and actions may very well be ones the teacher does not or cannot preconceive. The teacher does not define in advance what insights, understandings, and actions are hoped for, but may have to learn what true vision, appropriate understanding, and fitting action mean from the learners. In spite of the fact that the teacher directs learning, the teacher also learns from the learners. The teaching-learning process is profoundly mutual and participatory.

The fourth step in the teaching-learning process is to provide time and space for students to struggle on their own, and to take time out from their struggles with the encounters they have had and the guidance they have received. The interlude is a crucial phase of the learning process, and it must be built into the way in which one teaches. Learners need to be given time and space in which to wait, and be encouraged to use it.

Most people are usually in too much of a hurry to resolve conflicts. Because such conflicts are painful, and often involve suffering, we wish to escape them as quickly as possible. But this short-circuits the process. Waiting is an important part of learning. The teaching-learning process must involve acceptance and encouragement of prolonged periods of struggle and also of periods of seeming inactivity and lack of resolution. Because, to a certain extent, conflict, struggle, and the drive toward some form of resolution and interpretation are natural and daily occurrences, the affirmation and encouragement of waiting may be the most important thing we have to teach.

The teacher's role is to provide a context in which premature resolution of conflict is not demanded. It must be a context in which learners are given time to reflect, to leave some decisions unmade, and are not hurried into making premature commitments or public stands. The context must be a social environment in which learners are free and encouraged to pause and wait when appropriate, and a spatial context in which learners are able to move out of the center of attention when needed.

This important point is not always observed in other approaches to moral education. In an excellent critique of the values clarification approach, John S. Stewart argues that

> the demand for public affirmation and action which is such an important part of the VC philosophy ... is ... potentially dangerous, especially when one is working with teenagers. Research conducted by social psychologists has

revealed that when people take public positions or are forced to act they tend to cling to the beliefs or values involved, even if those beliefs or values are tentative or not genuinely held at the time of the commitment or action. . . . Premature affirmation or action, therefore, can be a very dangerous thing to induce. . . . During the important developmental years of adolescence and youth, there is a need for genuine commitment, rational action, and public affirmation. But the risks are also great, and such behaviors should not be artificially induced or prematurely generated.[9]

This same criticism can be made of Kohlberg's proposal that moral education should focus on persons' public presentations of solutions to dilemmas and of their comparisons with those of others. Very often people will just not have something to say publicly, either because they are still struggling inwardly or because they cannot yet find the right way to say what in some sense they know.

If learners are given the opportunity for encounter, are supported and encouraged in undergoing and exploring these encounters in such a way that their struggles are informed by images, words, and concepts that guide them, and are given time and space both to struggle and to wait, we may expect that they will come to new visions and understandings of their own that resolve these conflicts for them. If this happens, they will have something to say. They will want and need to interpret their experiences to themselves and to others. The role of the teacher at this point is to listen, to suggest possibilities of interpretation in expression and action, and to instruct and train learners in modes of interpretation—all, of course, in the context of a relationship that is deeply respectful of the learners' own insights and styles of interpretation, and without self-serving motivation on the part of the teacher. This is the final step in the teaching-learning process.

Interpretation in the teaching-learning process is the disciplined procedure of helping one another to find appropriate ways of expressing and understanding the encounters and explorations that have been undertaken. We make more or less systematic connections between our own conflicts, images, and resolutions and the experiences of others, using symbolic forms that communicate.

Interpretation involves give-and-take between teachers and learners. The teacher listens to the learners, who grope to express what they feel and mean. The teacher responds by asking whether this is meant or that, whether one learner's ways of saying things are or are not analogous to some other person's ways of saying things, and providing options for expression that may help the learners to say what is meant more clearly. The teacher must, of course, always allow and encourage the learners to say no if the teacher's suggestions are misleading.

The forms of expression used in the interpretation process may be quite varied. Interpretation may take the form of verbal or written dialogue between learners and teachers. Such dialogue may involve telling one another stories about one's experience. These may be autobiographical, linking past feelings, experiences, and understandings with present ones. They may also lead into the future, expressing hopes, dreams, visions, plans, and intentions. Such stories will be all the more helpful to the extent that they include deeper characterizations of the persons involved and metaphors that open up the story at levels beyond the informational and by means of which other persons can make analogical associations.

Storytelling is a most important form of interpretation, and one that is in practice quite often neglected. But it is not the only one. Other creative art forms also provide extremely important modes of interpretation. Interpretation in worship should not be neglected either. Hymns of adoration and praise; prayers of confession, thanksgiving, and intercession; the instruction of the scriptures and preaching; the focus on the life, love, sacrifice, and resurrection of Christ in the Lord's supper—all of these may provide the occasion for the expression of one's experience at profound levels.[10]

Not to be neglected here either are the more formalistic attempts to interpret moral experience and connect it with the experience of others through struggling toward and grappling with moral principles and rules. To some extent we may universalize aspects of our experience and call to our aid the universalizable aspects of the experience of others without losing the texture and complexity of our relations with the particularities of our own experience and the specificity of our own stories and traditions. When this is the case, we may, through moral principles and rules, be able to make fundamental connections between our own experiences and those of humankind as a whole.

Finally, in many cases, the most important and appropriate form of interpretation in the moral life is action. What we actually do for and with others speaks clearly to ourselves and to others about the nature and meaning of our conflicts and resolutions. In fact, many moral conflicts cannot be resolved without fitting action. The moral life ultimately manifests itself in the way in which we behave toward others. In the teaching-learning process, setting action in the context of the whole process helps people interpret what they have truly experienced and becomes a crucial indicator of the quality of our moral lives. Action, likewise, engages us with new conflicts in the context of which the process must be constantly repeated. Action as interpretation, however, means that action is not the sole concern of the moral life. It is a manifestation of the quality of our moral lives and a result of the moral progress we make by going through the whole process.

The teacher is a listener to, assistant in, collaborator with, and celebrator of the interpretations of the learners. The emphasis here has been on the interpretation of the encounters and explorations for which the teacher is to some extent responsible. However, learners will have encounters that they undergo and explore, and conflicts that they resolve, apart from the teaching-learning process. The teacher, through close attention to the learners, may sense that this has happened, and has a responsibility to listen carefully to what the learners have to say about these. The teacher's role in the interpretation process may begin here and be carried through. In this context, careful attention to the kinds of experiences related by Robinson earlier can be a very important feature of Christian education for the moral life.

These, then, are the kinds of things we as teachers can do to facilitate and guide moral learning in the Christian context. Teaching is at once an investigative process that leads learners to explore reality, a critical process that challenges them in the context of their own widening and deepening experience, a hermeneutical process that helps them interpret and see reality more clearly, and a caring process that facilitates their engagement with the world in repentance, attention, and service.

The analytical, critical, reflective dialogue between a learner and a teacher concerning experiences they have together is absolutely central and necessary for growth in the Christian moral life. In order to grow, we need teachers who show us around the world, hear what we have to say, and respond to that with compassion. But teaching does not go on in a vacuum. It grows in the rich soil of a community that teaches us to be receptive, attentive servants in the world. Only by living in such a community can we experience what these things mean and learn the disciplines of discipleship. The church as a whole provides the context for our growth as it lives intentionally and consciously in repentance, prayer, and service.

Through the Life Cycle

In spite of the fact that our view of moral progress is not strictly a developmental one, but rather one that sees moral growth as the activation of human capacities in the context of concrete personal circumstances and broad historical and cultural processes, we are not completely at a loss to chart out differences in approaches to moral education through the lifespan. The basic strategy and purpose remain constant. But, because at different times in people's lives different issues predominate and different intellectual and emotional capacities are available to shape and deal with those issues, there are differences of emphasis in the teaching-learning process as persons move through the various natural stages and life phases.

In early childhood, the child lives in a world constituted at one pole by intimate relations with a small number of loved ones on whom the child utterly depends, and at another pole by a strange world full of the unfamiliar and unknown. Between these two poles the realms of the neighbor and the enemy come into being. Strangers become neighbors or enemies as they are encountered on the basis of secure or insecure relations with loved ones. The less secure the relations with the loved ones, the more strangers remain strangers or become enemies. The more secure the relations with the loved ones, the more the realm of the stranger can be explored and the more strangers become neighbors. The time of childhood is primarily a time of exploring a strange world in its concreteness. Throughout childhood, neighbors and enemies multiply out of encounters with many strangers. Whether strangers usually tend to become neighbors or enemies makes a profound impact on a child's moral life.

Because children cannot see ahead of childhood, children live in the moment and focus on the immediate. In some ways, this is an advantage for the moral life. Although children cannot apprehend the many aspects of reality simultaneously, a child's apprehension of the concrete and immediate may be penetratingly insightful and frightfully clear. A conventional picture of reality has not yet been learned. Children seem to have a natural capacity to become fully absorbed in a concrete reality. Things that seem ordinary to adolescents and adults often seem to a child to be deep and inexhaustible mysteries. Such concentration on the concrete and the apprehension of mystery are qualities of secure childhood that must be retained in the mature moral life in the context of abstract conceptual abilities.

Children live through play and imagery. They lack the ability in many instances to differentiate the imaginal world from the "real" world. The child's world is, in part, a world of make-believe and fairy tales. Many developmental psychologists argue that we must grow out of this entirely in order to see the world as it is. And, as C. Daniel Batson has argued: "Few Christian educators would be willing to have Bible stories treated lightly as fairy tales."[11]

But just as children come to see reality through play, albeit in a sometimes dangerously concrete way, we need to allow children to use religious language in a playful way. After all, is the Gospel really so far from fairy tale as we often think? Frederick Buechner, a novelist and Presbyterian minister, suggests that it is not. The fairy-tale world, he says,

> is a world of magic and mystery, of deep darkness and flickering starlight. It is a world where terrible things happen and wonderful things too. It is a world where goodness is pitted against evil, love against hate, order against chaos, in a great struggle where often it is hard to be sure who belongs to which side because appearances are endlessly deceptive. Yet for all its confusion and wildness,

it is a world where the battle goes ultimately to the good, who live happily ever after, and where in the long run everybody, good and evil alike, becomes known by his true name.[12]

That is the gospel, this meeting of darkness and light in the final victory of light. That is the fairy tale of the Gospel with, of course, the one crucial difference from all other fairy tales, which is that the claim made for it is that it is true, that it not only happened once upon a time but has kept on happening ever since and is happening still.[13]

The fairy-tale world is very different from the ordinary world, but it may not be very far away. "It is as if the world of the fairy tale impinges on the ordinary world the way the dimension of depth impinges on the two-dimensional surface of a plane, so that there is no point on the plane . . . that can't become an entrance to it."[14] If this is true, then children's believing the Gospel even as fairy tale is not a danger at all. It may be just the form of play they need in order for them to see reality in depth and as mystery ultimately ordered toward the goodness of God.

One Sunday, returning home from church, I was having the typical what-did-you-do-in-Sunday-school-today conversation with my two sons. The younger, who was six, came up with this: "My teacher, we made bread together and I ate mine already and it was good." My son had learned that the people of the Bible made bread themselves, and that making bread was important for their life together. He had also learned, through his own experience, that he could make bread with people at church and that it was good. He had "played" with the people of the Bible, "played" with his teacher and his classmates, "played" with bread, and "played" with the images that bring all these together. He ate it all and found it good.[15]

Moral learning during childhood involves the exploration of broader worlds through actual encounters and of deeper worlds through imaginal processes. The primary teaching tasks are establishing a secure relationship with children, introducing children to appropriate new encounters with the world, presenting symbolic forms that draw children imaginally deeper into reality, supporting and guiding children in their struggles to understand and respond to new realities, listening to children's interpretations of their experience, and providing media and the training to use them so that their interpretations can be expressed in a variety of ways.

Adolescence is often celebrated as a time of great moral achievement. It is a time for many when formal operational thought and the ability to take the roles of others and do "social reasoning" in a complex way become available. It is a time when persons are shaping an identity and appropriating personal values. It is a time of idealism and great expectations.

The development of such capacities and the exigency of such psychosocial tasks may, however, also occasion great moral darkness. Philip Haillie reflects on this experience in his own life:

> I keep finding that I have been immoral when I have been incapable of awareness. Just as simple as that. I have been immoral in proportion to my incapacity for awareness . . . . When have I been more aware, and when have I been less aware of the human soul, mine or other people's? In my youth I was so unaware not only of other human souls, compared to the way I am now, or hope to think I am now, but also sublimely unaware of the heart of darkness in my own soul.[16]

Formal operational thinking opens up the immense world of abstract possibility. But the new availability of such possibilities on the horizon of youth may lead young people to almost complete lack of attention to the concrete. Idealism of youth tends to "soar above existence, out of contact with its conditions," says Donald Vandenberg, reporting the ideas of Romano Guardini, the German theologian, psychologist, and educator.[17]

> Thus the temporal structure of youth is future-laden. The preparation for success in terms of acquiring knowledge and therewith power seems relatively unnecessary because ideas and character are overrated. The lack of experience signifies that youth has no idea what he can do, what others are able to do, or what in general can be done: he

lacks awareness of the tenacity of facticity, that factuality that inheres in the human condition. He lacks awareness of the uncontrollability of human affairs. He lives for the future, but exuberantly, over-expectantly.[18]

Furthermore, youth is a period in which there is usually more self-concern than at any other time in the life cycle. At no other time is the establishment and security of the self necessarily so deeply in question. Most of the energies of the self are directed toward self-establishment and self-securing. In adolescence, more than at any other time, people use others as mirrors in which to see themselves. This is why solidified peer groups and uncomplicated ideologies are so important and attractive to youth. Adolescence is noted for stereotyping and conventionality, even if the particular conventions young persons adopt seem unconventional from an adult point of view.

In such circumstances, making the movements of repentance, prayer, and service, or being truly receptive and attentive to concrete persons as inexhaustible particulars, becomes most difficult. Mysteries are constantly reduced to problems in order that the adolescent may confirm in the self the power to handle reality. But this is also the period during which a self in the fullest sense is beginning to cohere, a self that may intentionally and consciously be given over in receptivity and attention to others in the context of a world more complex than the world of a child.

For the adolescent, the self is the most magnetic object of personal concern. The task of adolescence is to come to see this self more and more realistically. The irony of this life phase, however, is that this is done more adequately to the extent that the self is less a direct object of one's attentive energies. Youth need increasingly to use their new abilities to attend to objects outside of themselves. As Murdoch says, "It is attachment to what lies outside the fantasy mechanism, and not the mechanism itself, that liberates."[19]

The primary role of the teacher of adolescents is now, more than at any other time, that of a sure guide to the truth and value of the realities that youth encounter. But also, and perhaps more importantly than at any other time, this guidance must not be authoritarian. Adolescence is often a period of almost overwhelming internal and interpersonal conflict. What the adolescent needs is a safe place in which to struggle. The teacher must be fully present in order both to do battle against the adolescent and to affirm the adolescent as a fellow-struggler. The helpful moral teacher will be one who can both love and struggle with adolescents at the same time, critiquing their limitations and affirming their strivings, drawing them outward while allowing them inwardness, all in a constant dialectic.

Adulthood is the life phase in which the value of the concrete, the daily, the ordinary may reappear. In adulthood, we increasingly recognize that we live in particular places and times, and not in all places and times. We come to realize that it is here that our moral lives must be lived. This can lead to moral despair over the limitations of our own and others' concreteness, but it may alternatively lead into the depths of the concrete.

In adulthood we start all over again, in a sense. We may regain interest in the concrete and in imaginal apprehensions of its depth. But as we do so, we do it all differently. We do it in a much more complex and confusing world, one that includes the future and the past as well as the present, the abstract as well as the concrete, the facticity of existence as known through reflection as well as through immediate experience. In this context, the full movements of repentance, prayer, and service become possible because we know what is at stake, that is, the whole self and the whole world, not just as it is lived, but also as it is known. In this context, one assumes responsibility for one's own involvement in the process of moral growth in all its dimensions. Furthermore, one assumes responsibility for the moral growth and education of others. Here the stake in seeing clearly and interpreting rightly in expression and action is most dramatically revealed.

Throughout the life cycle, then, the creative process of moral learning may take place. But it takes different shapes, depending on the needs and abilities of the learners, and some of these are developmentally established. The experience of the repenting, praying, and serving community is investigated, shared, and taken responsibility for in different ways at different ages and stages. It is most fully experienced, however, only in adulthood.

Conclusion

"We live in a world whose mystery transcends us and . . . morality is the exploration of that mystery in so far as it concerns each individual."[20] This affirmation has guided our investigations as we have sought to determine what it means to be moral in the context of Christian faith, what is involved in moral growth, and what the church might do to educate for the Christian moral life. We found that becoming moral is a matter of undertaking the disciplines of repentance, prayer, and service. As we do so, we find ourselves increasingly transformed by God's grace, so that our receptivity, attention, and compassion for all reality may grow. There are things we can do together to help each other to come into a position where we can be so transformed. What we do is to live in the context of a repenting, praying, and serving community—investigating, sharing, and taking responsibility for our experiences there. This is what it means to do Christian education for the moral life. We do it so that the mystery of reality may be revealed to us all, and in order that we may respond to that mystery as responsible disciples.

Notes

Introduction

1. The terms "juridical ethics" and visional ethics" are my own. The distinction is made in analogous ways, however, by others. See, especially, the way in which "decisionism" and "an ethics of character" are contrasted by James W. McClendon in *Biography as Theology* (Nashville: Abingdon Press, 1974), chap. 1; and H. Richard Niebuhr's distinction between the master image of "man-the-citizen" and "the responsible self" in *The Responsible Self* (New York: Harper & Row, 1963), chap. 1.

I use the term "juridical" to pick up both the emphasis on decisions that McClendon highlights and the political and legal quality of this form of ethics that Niebuhr's image underscores. I use the term "visional" for different reasons. I find the notions of "character" and "responsibility" that McClendon and Niebuhr use to label the alternative to be both significant and related. But more fundamental than either is the matter of vision. As I will try to show in Chapter 2, character grows out of vision and vision is what makes responsibility possible.

Visional ethics has an ancient history, but it has been obscured by the hegemony of juridical ethics since the Enlightenment. The principal contemporary thinker to articulate the centrality of vision in the moral life is the Oxford moral philosopher and novelist Iris Murdoch. Her work has been my primary guide in developing both my critique of current theory in moral development and education and my alternative. Her ideas have, however, also influenced another source from which I draw heavily: Stanley Hauerwas, a Protestant Christian ethicist who teaches at Notre Dame University and who builds his "character ethics" partly on Murdoch's contributions. These two, together with H. Richard Niebuhr, whose own unique dealings with the theme of vision in relation to responsibility I try to develop, are the main members of the family of thinkers I draw on in attempting to describe the visional alternative to juridical ethics.

2. Philosophers in the juridical tradition have striven mightily to establish "the institution of morality" on independent grounds. Morality, they say, if it is to impinge in a like way on all persons, must be independent

of the relativisms of different religions and religious points of view. It must be universal, and therefore *sui generis.* The struggle has been to search out the independent, autonomous, and universal elements in the moral life, and to structure around them an understanding of what morality is. There has been a general consensus in juridical ethics that this element is what might be called "the right rule of reason." Reason is the root of morality, and that which all "reasonable" people can agree is right *is* right. Reason is seen to be independent of religious belief or conviction. If the will of God corresponds to the right rule of reason, then it is right. But the basis for the morality of the judgment is not the fact that God wills it, but its rationality. Therefore, any reasonable person may be moral. Reference to a person's religious life is, at this point, irrelevant. The moral life thus becomes essentially independent of the religious life.

The high view of reason found in juridical ethics is supported by the high view of reason found in cognitive-developmental psychology. Piaget is the first to articulate this connection clearly. For Piaget, mature morality is above all "a conscious realization of the logic of relations between persons" (*The Moral Judgment of the Child* [New York: Collier Books, 1966], p. 403). It is a matter of learning the rules of the game of cooperative interpersonal relationships and the higher-order principles that govern it. Being moral means getting a rational grip on a system of relationships and operating within it to achieve cognitive equilibrium.

These two thrusts converge more explicitly and powerfully in Kohlberg's work than anywhere else, since he both builds on the Piagetian developmental model and carries out a prolonged philosophical argument for his conception of morality.

3. The present study is not an introduction to Kohlberg's work. The first chapter, especially, presupposes some knowledge of what Kohlberg has formulated. One good introduction to Kohlberg is Ronald Duska and Mariellen Whelan, *Moral Development: A Guide to Piaget and Kohlberg* (New York: Paulist Press, 1975). Part III of *Moral Education . . . It Comes with the Territory,* David Purpel and Kevin Ryan, eds. (Berkeley, Calif.: McCutchan Publishing Corp., 1976) contains two introductory articles by Kohlberg to his theories, plus some helpful review essays and critiques by others.

Chapter One

1. See Lawrence Kohlberg, "Education for Justice: A Modern Statement of the Platonic View," in *Moral Education: Five Lectures,* ed. T. R. Sizer and N. F. Sizer (Cambridge, Mass.: Harvard University Press, 1970),

p. 58, and idem, "From Is to Ought: How to Commit the Naturalistic Fallacy and Get Away with It," in *Cognitive Development and Epistemology*, ed. T. Mischel (New York: Academic Press, 1971), p. 210.

2. See Lawrence Kohlberg, "Stage and Sequence: The Cognitive-Developmental Approach to Socialization," in *Handbook of Socialization Theory and Research*, ed. D. Goslin (New York: Rand McNally, 1969), pp. 349, 398.

3. Cf. ibid., p. 352.

4. See Kohlberg, "From Is to Ought," p. 224

5. William F. Alston, "Comments on Kohlberg," in Mischel, *Cognitive Development and Epistemology*, pp. 276–77.

6. See Kohlberg, "From Is to Ought," p. 232, and idem, "Education for Justice," *passim*.

7. See Plato, *Protagoras*, 330b.

8. For a technical argument on Plato's understanding of the unity of the virtues, see Gregory Vlastos, *Platonic Studies* (Princeton: Princeton University Press, 1973), chap. 10.

9. Kenneth Keniston, "Moral Development, Youthful Activism, and Modern Society," *The Critic* 28 (1969): 23.

10. For an excellent, brief description of the relation of the virtue of justice to other virtues, see Ralph B. Potter, "Justice and Beyond in Moral Education," *Andover Newton Quarterly* 19 (January 1979): 151.

11. Lawrence Kohlberg, "Stages of Moral Development as a Basis for Moral Education," in *Moral Education: Interdisciplinary Approaches*, ed. C. M. Beck, B. S. Crittenden, and E. V. Sullivan (New York: Newman Press, 1971), p. 58.

12. See Lawrence Kohlberg, "The Claim to Moral Adequacy of a Highest Stage of Moral Judgment," *The Journal of Philosophy* 70 (1973): 643, where Kohlberg states the procedure in the following way:

1. To imagine oneself in each person's position in that situation (including the self) and to consider all the claims he could make (or which the self could make in his position).

2. Then to imagine that the individual does not know which person he is in the situation and to ask whether he would still uphold that claim.

3. Then to act in accordance with these reversible claims in the situation.

13. Johannes Pedersen, *Israel: Its Life and Culture,* vol. II (London: Oxford University Press, 1926), p. 373.

14. Iris Murdoch, "The Sublime and the Good," *Chicago Review* 13 (1959): 42.

15. A reading of Robert Coles's studies of the rural poor and of the participants in the civil rights movement provides many examples of such people. See, for a few, Coles, "A House of Truth," *The American Scholar* 34 (Autumn 1965): 620–25.

16. Kohlberg, "The Claim to Moral Adequacy," p. 641.

17. Charles Taylor, "What Is Involved in Genetic Psychology?" in Mischel, *Cognitive Development and Epistemology,* p. 410.

18. Carol Gilligan, in a study on how people deal with actual moral dilemmas, states that the students she studied "often reported their discovery that principles of justice did not encompass the complexity of the moral problems they faced. Such principles, in fact, were often found to coexist with feelings of intolerance that limited knowledge of both self and others. One student concluded that his claim to an objectively principled moral truth had distanced him in a relationship with a woman and blinded him to the realization of what—from her perspective—was going on. Then the claim to an absolute moral judgment was seen to depend on 'staying really far apart from people' or 'hardening yourself to people you are really close to' and ignoring the reality of more distant suffering" ("Justice and Responsibility: Thinking about Real Dilemmas of Moral Conflict and Choice," in *Toward Moral and Religious Maturity: The First International Conference on Moral and Religious Development,* Christiane Brusselmans, convenor [Morristown, N.J.: Silver Burdett Co., 1980], p. 241).

19. Bill Puka, "Moral Education and Its Cure," in *Reflections on Values Education,* ed. J. Meyer (Waterloo, Ont.: Wilfrid Laurier University Press, 1976), pp. 60–61.

20. Coles, "A House of Truth," p. 622.

21. Ibid., p. 624.

22. Taylor, "What Is Involved in Genetic Psychology?," p. 411.

23. Ibid., p. 413.

24. Ibid.

25. Cf. Martin L. Hoffman, "The Development of Altruistic Motivation," in *Moral Development: Current Theory and Research,* D. J. DePalma and J. M. Foley (Hillsdale, N.J.: Lawrence Erlbaum Associates, 1975), p. 148.

26. Roger R. Straughan, "Hypothetical Moral Dilemmas," *Journal of Moral Education* 4 (1975): 184.

27. Iris Murdoch, "Vision and Choice in Morality," in *Christian Ethics and Contemporary Philosophy,* ed. I. Ramsey (New York: Macmillan, 1966), p. 202.

28. Ibid., p. 203.

29. Ibid.

30. James W. McClendon, *Biography as Theology* (Nashville: Abingdon Press, 1974), p. 19.

31. Iris Murdoch, *The Sovereignty of Good* (New York: Schocken Books, 1970), p. 36.

32. Lawrence Kohlberg, "Moral Education, Religious Education, and the Public School: A Developmental View," in *Religion and Public Education,* ed. T. Sizer (Boston: Houghton Mifflin Co., 1967), pp. 180, 181.

33. Lawrence Kohlberg, "Education, Moral Development, and Faith," *Journal of Moral Education* 4 (1974): 11.

34. See James Fowler, "Mapping Faith's Structures: A Developmental Overview," in *Life Maps: The Human Journey of Faith,* ed. J. Berryman (Waco, Tex.: Word Books, 1978), chap. 1. Fowler discusses the relation of his stages to Kohlberg's in a recent chapter, "Moral Stages and the Development of Faith," in *Moral Development, Moral Education, and Kohlberg,* ed. B. Munsey (Birmingham, Ala.: Religious Education Press, 1980), pp. 130–60.

35. Kohlberg, "Education, Moral Development, and Faith," pp. 13–14.

36. Ibid., p. 14.

37. Ibid.

38. Ibid.

39. Ibid.

Chapter Two

1. Iris Murdoch, "Vision and Choice in Morality," in *Christian Ethics and Contemporary Philosophy,* ed. I. Ramsey (New York: Macmillan, 1966), p. 208.

2. Iris Murdoch, "Against Dryness: A Polemical Sketch," *Encounter* 16 (1961): 20.

3. G. S. Hendry, "Mystery," in *A Theological Word Book of the Bible,* ed. A. Richardson (New York: Macmillan, 1960), p. 156.

4. Gabriel Marcel, *Mystery of Being,* vol. I, trans. G. F. Fraser (Chicago: Henry Regnery Co., 1960), p. 260.

5. See above, pp. 19 and 21.

6. Marcel, *Mystery of Being,* p. 260.

7. Ibid., p. 261.

8. Iris Murdoch, "The Sublime and the Beautiful Revisited," *The Yale Review* 49 (1959): 259–60.

9. G. K. Chesterton, *Orthodoxy* (Garden City, N.Y.: Image Books, 1959), p. 132.

10. Iris Murdoch, "The Sublime and the Good," *Chicago Review* 13 (1959): 54.

11. Ibid., p. 51.

12. Stanley Hauerwas, "Character, Narrative, and Growth in the Christian Life," in *Toward Moral and Religious Maturity: The First International Conference on Moral and Religious Development,* Christiane Brusselmans, convenor (Morristown, N.J.: Silver Burdett Co., 1980), pp. 463–64.

13. Cf. Diogenes Allen, *Finding Our Father* (Atlanta: John Knox Press, 1974), chap. 2, where the author explains how love for another being involves regarding that being as a particularity. Also, in a footnote (n. 15, pp. 118–19), Allen explains the meaning of particularity. It is:

> the recognition of the reality of things independently of the distortion caused by our perception of them from our own point of view. To perceive things independently of our tastes, desires, preferences, and of their utility—in short, to release them from our orbit—is to perceive them as particulars. In other words, to see ourselves as but one reality among many others, is to recognize them as particulars; it is to recognize their particularity.
>
> The justification of this usage is that one way in which we can control others, or put them into orbit around ourselves, is by classifying them according to type: see a thing as a chair, or a person as a neurotic. Their particular reality can thus be lost in the *general* type, and we then do not notice that though they can be so viewed and reduced, they can break these bounds and can be seen as themselves.

To so reduce them is, of course, precisely the opposite of what it means to love them.

14. Iris Murdoch, *The Sovereignty of Good* (New York: Schocken Books, 1970), p. 66.

15. Lawrence Kohlberg, "From Is to Ought," in Mischel, *Cognitive Development and Epistemology,* pp. 214–15, and idem, "Stages of Moral Development," in Beck, *Moral Education,* p. 56.

16. Murdoch, p. 80.

17. Ibid., pp. 62–63.

18. It is interesting to note that in the same passage Jesus admonishes

the rich man for calling him good. He says, "No one is good except God alone" (Mark 10:18), including himself. In other words, the Good is transcendent.

19. Iris Murdoch, "Metaphysics and Ethics," in *The Nature of Metaphysics,* ed. D. T. Pears (London: Macmillan, 1967), p. 113.

20. Murdoch, *Sovereignty of Good,* p. 35.

21. Ibid., p. 84.

22. Walker Percy, *Love in the Ruins* (New York: Avon Books, 1971), p. 144.

23. Gabriel Marcel, *Homo Viator,* trans. E. Craufurd (New York: Harper and Row, 1962), pp. 17–18.

24. Ibid., p. 19.

25. Ibid. For another, and very illuminating, analysis of the problem of moral egocentricity, see Allen, *Finding Our Father,* especially chap. 2.

26. Murdoch, *Sovereignty of Good,* p. 38.

27. Kohlberg, "Education for Justice," in Sizer and Sizer, *Moral Education,* p. 63.

28. Paul L. Holmer, *C. S. Lewis: The Shape of His Faith and Thought* (New York: Harper & Row, 1976), p. 88.

29. Ibid., p. 90.

30. C. S. Lewis, *An Experiment in Criticism* (Cambridge: Cambridge University Press, 1961), p. 17.

31. James M. Gustafson has a fine essay on the relation of vision and character entitled "Moral Discernment in the Christian Life," which is found in his *Theology and Christian Ethics* (Philadelphia: United Church Press, 1974), chap. 5. Although he does not use the term "character" as a summarizing concept, he notes that "it is persons who discern; and persons have histories that affect their discernment" (p. 107). The essay is an attempt to unravel a number of the complex features involved in these histories which make us who we are and affect our vision.

32. "The Self as Story" is chapter 4 in Hauerwas's *Vision and Virtue* (Notre Dame: Fides Publications, 1974).

33. Hauerwas, *Vision and Virtue,* p. 74.

34. James W. McClendon, *Biography as Theology* (Nashville: Abingdon Press, 1974), p. 34.

35. Cf. James W. McClendon, Jr. and James M. Smith, *Understanding Religious Convictions* (Notre Dame: University of Notre Dame Press, 1975), pp. 91–92.

36. Stanley Hauerwas, *Truthfulness and Tragedy* (Notre Dame: University of Notre Dame Press, 1977), p. 28.

37. Dag Hammarskjöld, "Old Creeds in a New World," in Henry P.

Van Dusen, *Dag Hammarskjöld: The Statesman and His Faith* (New York: Harper & Row, 1967), pp. 46–47.

38. Hauerwas, *Vision and Virtue,* p. 46.

39. Quoted from Max Weber, "Politics as a Vocation" by Carol Gilligan, "Justice and Responsibility," in *Toward Moral and Religious Maturity,* p. 246.

40. As Murdoch puts it: "If I attend properly I will have no choices and this is the ultimate condition to be aimed at" (*Sovereignty of Good,* 40). "We act rightly 'when the time comes' not out of strength of will but out of the quality of our usual attachments and with the kind of energy and discernment which we have available. And to this the whole activity of our consciousness is relevant" (pp. 91–92).

41. See H. Richard Niebuhr, *The Responsible Self* (New York: Harper & Row, 1963), pp. 61–65.

42. Ibid., p. 61.

43. Ibid., p. 63.

44. Ibid., p. 64.

45. Ibid., p. 65.

Chapter Three

1. Jacques Lusseyran, *And There Was Light,* trans. E. R. Cameron (Boston: Little, Brown and Company, 1963), p. 8. Cf. Dorothee Soelle's treatment of Lusseyran's story in her *Suffering,* trans. E. R. Kalin (Philadelphia: Fortress Press, 1975), pp. 88–93. Soelle's book first brought my attention to Lusseyran's book and to these particular passages.

2. Quoted in Soelle, *Suffering,* p. 222.

3. Edward Robinson's research, however, has demonstrated that a great many more people have had such experiences than we would ordinarily expect. As director of the Religious Experience Research Unit at Manchester College, Oxford, Robinson and his predecessor, Sir Alister Hardy, have collected over 4,000 firsthand accounts of these kinds of experiences, many of which took place during childhood. I believe that many of these experiences can be understood as experiences of imaginal transformation of the kind I wish to describe in this chapter. One of the accounts that Robinson provided goes as follows:

> As a child of eight, wandering alone on ... Hill ... and as I began to be afraid, I realized that I was not alone. An elderly gentleman from the village, a Mr. S., who was said to have a famous collection of moths and butterflies, and who always wore black gloves, was bending over a juniper bush with his net. Partly

because of the gloves, partly because of his part in local noncon-
formist politics with my father . . . Mr. S. was to me the personifica-
tion of evil and the unknown. I was frozen. Suddenly the sun shone
out behind the thunderhead, sending its rays down over the landscape. I knew much better than to think that God was "up there,"
though I was aware, from picture books, of the symbol. But
suddenly I *knew* that there was light in dark places; and I experienced a security in the face of which evil palled. I have never been
totally afraid again (and I was around a bit in the War). And
suddenly, too, I knew that this was just a rather pathetic, lonely
old man, and that I *loved* him. (Quoted in Edward Robinson, "I
Called It 'It,' " *Faith and Freedom* 25 [1972]: 151.)

In an article entitled "Education and Unreality" (*Learning for Living* 16
[1976]: 162–67), Robinson suggests that these experiences have four basic
characteristics. First, these are experiences of "an immediate apprehension
of reality" (p. 164). Second, they can be experienced at any age, "come
independently of verbal expression or operational thinking," and "are absolutely beyond reason to deny or confirm" (p. 164). Third, they are "marked
not only by a sense of reality but a sense of something that reality requires. . ." (p. 166). And fourth, they are experiences to which in times of
crisis, when convention and even reason seem inadequate to help us chart
our course, "we turn, not with feelings of nostalgia, a sentimental desire to
return to a past long dead, but with the feeling that there at least was, is, a
certainty that is still meaningful" (p. 166).

4. Edward Robinson, "Experience and Authority in Religious Education," *Religious Education* 71 (1976): 458.

5. Charles Taylor, "What Is Involved in Genetic Psychology?" in
Mischel, *Cognitive Development and Epistemology*, p. 415.

6. John C. Gibbs, "Kohlberg's Stages of Moral Development: A
Constructive Critique," *Harvard Educational Review* 47 (1977): 47.

7. Gibbs has argued that Kohlberg's highest two stages are not really
natural developmental stages at all, but rather "formalizations which are
based on the achievements of the natural stages and which proceed on a
reflective and philosophical plane of discourse" (ibid., p. 56).

8. Michael Foster, *Mystery and Philosophy* (London: SCM Press,
1957), p. 71.

9. This story is published in *The Complete Stories of Flannery O'Connor*, ed. Robert Giroux (New York: Farrar, Straus and Giroux, 1979), pp.
488–509. All of the quotations in this section are taken from these pages.

10. Iris Murdoch, *The Sovereignty of Good* (New York: Schocken Books, 1970), p. 52.

11. H. Richard Niebuhr, *The Responsible Self* (New York: Harper & Row, 1963), pp. 151–52.

12. Mary Warnock, *Imagination* (Berkeley: University of California Press, 1976), p. 196.

13. James E. Loder, *Religious Pathology and Christian Faith* (Philadelphia: Westminster Press, 1966), p. 142.

14. There is a strong similarity here to the process of "accommodation and assimilation" discussed by Piaget and Kohlberg. The differences have to do with the way in which I locate this primarily in the imagination and the emphasis I give to the ongoing dynamic of this process in all of its dimensions rather than on the particular structural formations it may resolve into for a time with regard to certain aspects of reality (i.e., space, time, causality, reciprocity, etc.).

15. Iris Murdoch, "The Sublime and the Good," *Chicago Review* 13 (1959): 52.

16. H. Richard Niebuhr, *The Meaning of Revelation* (New York: The Macmillan Co., 1960), p. 72. See also pp. 73–74, where Niebuhr provides a variety of examples of evil imagination. William F. Lynch's *Images of Hope* (Baltimore: Helicon Press, 1965) is another helpful resource on the uses of imagination. He contrasts "the realistic and human imagination," defined as "the sum total of all the forces and faculties in man that are brought to bear upon our concrete world to form proper images of it" (p. 243), with what he calls "fantasy." He says, "The first task of such an imagination . . . is to find a way through fantasy and lies into fact and existence. The second task of such an imagination is to create perspective for the facts it has found" (p. 243). Lynch's book as a whole, though concerned primarily with the way in which the imagination plays a primary healing function in the life of mentally ill people, works out a perspective with which my own thoughts on moral growth are entirely sympathetic. Persons who wish to pursue this perspective will gain immeasurably from reading Lynch's book.

17. O'Connor makes this clear as she writes: "There was an instant when she was certain that she was about to be in an earthquake. All at once her vision narrowed and she saw everything as if it were happening in a small room far away, or as if she were looking at it though the wrong end of a telescope." Then, moments later, "Mrs. Turpin's vision suddenly reversed itself and she saw everything large instead of small" ("Revelation," p. 499).

18. Niebuhr, *Meaning of Revelation,* p. 80.

19. Ibid.

20. My sources for the pattern are primarily Harold Rugg, *Imagination: An Inquiry into the Sources and Conditions That Stimulate Creativity,* (New York: Harper & Row, 1963), and Loder, *Religious Pathology and Christian Faith.* Rugg's book is primarily a study of the dynamics and function of the imagination in creative thought and discovery in science and the arts. Loder makes use of Rugg's work (along with that of Kierkegaard and Freud) to study the dynamics and function of the imagination in religious growth and transformation. The basic paradigm that I am about to describe is one that both Loder and Rugg agree on and appeal to.

21. See Rugg, *Imagination,* pp. 290–91.

22. Ibid., p. 289.

23. Kohlberg's juridical ethics assumes that we always know what the problem is, where it is located, and who is involved when we experience conflict in the moral life. Often, however, we do not. Frequently, we sense tension but are simply baffled as to its source. Many times what appears to be the central problem is merely a symptom of a deeper and more extensive conflict. Usually we do not realize that this is the case until the deeper conflict is resolved and the more superficial difficulties just seem to disappear. The process we are describing in this section is one that makes room for this very typical, but hardly noticed, phenomenon. Part of what we discover in our discovery process is the difficulties we have worked through without even knowing it.

24. There is, at this point, an important agreement between what we have been saying and Kohlberg's contention that the impetus for moral development lies in our experiences of cognitive dissonance and intrapsychic conflict. The morally important results of dealing with such conflicts are limited by Kohlberg, however, to movement to higher stages of cognitive reasoning. We are concerned with results more broadly experienced. They ramify not just into cognitive structures, but also into our imaginal schemes and through them into our whole complex patterns of seeing, feeling, interpreting, valuing, and acting.

I wish to be clear, also, that agreement with Kohlberg on the importance of intrapsychic conflict in moral growth does not commit us to the "decisionist fallacy" in which the moral life is chopped up into isolated conflictual situations or problems. The conflicts with which we must deal can sometimes be focused situationally, but we bring to such situations the ongoing conflicts that we are perennially dealing with as moral beings. Conflicts within our own character, structural conflicts within broad social systems, and historical conflicts between peoples are among the dimensions of conflict with which we must deal continually in every situation. They perdure over time and manifest themselves in various ways in a variety of contexts. When we speak of engaging conflict, we do not speak of isolated, context-free, independently resolvable conflicts, but conflict as engaged in the complex web of interconnected human reality.

25. Lynch, *Images of Hope*, pp. 177–78.

26. See Loder, *Religious Pathology*, Section II.

27. Ibid., p. 193.

28. Ibid.

29. Niebuhr, *Meaning of Revelation*, p. 80.

Chapter Four

1. Diogenes Allen, *Between Two Worlds* (Atlanta: John Knox Press, 1977), pp. 14–15.

2. I began to consider these three disciplines as fundamental to the moral life of Christians in reflecting on Michael Foster's suggestions that the apprehension of mystery requires revelation and that revelation in turn presupposes repentance, the church, and prayer (*Mystery and Philosophy* [London: SCM Press, 1957], p. 82).

3. Jean Calvin, *The Institutes of the Christian Religion* III.3.5.

4. Donald Evans, *Struggle and Fulfillment* (Cleveland: William Collins Publishers, Inc., 1979), p. 21. See Introduction and Part One for Evans's full description of this struggle.

5. Ibid., p. 6.

6. Ibid. See Chapter Seven for a full discussion of this struggle.

7. Donald Evans, "Does Religious Faith Conflict with Moral Freedom?" in *Religion and Morality*, eds. G. Outka and J. P. Reeder, Jr. (Garden City, N.Y.: Anchor Books, 1973), p. 105.

8. Ibid., p. 358.

9. Simone Weil, *Waiting for God*, trans. E. Craufurd (New York: Harper & Row, 1973), p. 105.

10. Brother Lawrence, *The Practice of the Presence of God*, trans. and ed. D. Attwater (London: Burns Oates and Washbourne, Ltd., 1926), pp. 29–30.

11. Iris Murdoch, *The Sovereignty of Good* (New York: Schocken Books, 1970), p. 55.

12. Ibid.

13. Ibid., p. 56.

14. This, of course, works both ways. Evil is just as able to absorb our

attention as good, and can just as easily give us energy and claim our obedience. One of our great difficulties, unfortunately, is telling the difference between what is good and what is not. Evil is often more attractive, dazzling, and compelling than good, which can often seem quite boring and mundane. See Allen, *Between Two Worlds*, pp. 17–18.

15. Weil, *Waiting for God*, p. 105.

16. Ibid., pp. 109–10.

17. Ibid., p. 111.

18. Ibid., p. 130.

19. Murdoch, *Sovereignty of Good*, p. 101.

20. Ibid.

21. See Mt. 20:20–28, Mt. 23:11, Mk. 9:33–35, Mk. 10: 35–44, and Lk. 22: 24–27.

22. Weil, *Waiting for God*, p. 147.

23. See Hauerwas's discussion of this issue in his "The Politics of Charity," *Interpretation* 31 (1977): 251–62; reprinted in Hauerwas, *Tragedy and Truthfulness* (Notre Dame: University of Notre Dame Press, 1977), pp. 132–43.

24. Weil, *Waiting for God*, p. 48.

25. In defining service in this way, I have put the emphasis on service as interpersonal. This has the significant disadvantage of implying that service is relevant only to one-on-one personal relationships, and has no relevance to our political or institutional life. This is a disadvantage because it is clear that service cannot be limited to dealing with the effects of evil forces on the limited number of persons whom we encounter. Service has a political and prophetic dimension that aims at structures of evil and the causes of human suffering. But in order to deal with this dimension, it would be necessary to indulge in at least as extensive an analysis as we have already taken up, and it is impossible to do this here.

The dilemma of the relation of power and effectiveness to service in political service is, however, even more entangled than it is with regard to personal service. In fact, many would maintain that the idea of service as presence is utterly irrelevant to political service since politics is by definition the manipulation of power. I believe, however, that an understanding of political service can be worked out in a coherent way that retains the dynamics of vulnerability, equality, and compassion at its center. Some beginnings in this direction can be found in Hauerwas, "The Politics of Charity," and in several works by John H. Yoder, including *The Christian Witness to the State* (Newton: Faith and Life Press, 1964) and *The Politics of Jesus* (Grand Rapids: Eerdmans, 1973).

26. Weil, *Waiting for God*, p. 111.

27. Erik Erikson, *Toys and Reasons* (New York: W. W. Norton & Co., 1977), p. 46.

28. Ibid., p. 50.

29. See Jean Piaget, *Play, Dreams, and Imitation in Childhood,* trans. C. Gattengo and F. M. Hodgson (New York: W. W. Norton & Co., 1962), pp. 277–84.

30. Edward A. Robinson, "The Poet and the Policeman" (Unpublished address given to the Christian Education Movement Conference on Religious Education and the Imagination, Wrexham, England, April, 1975; mimeographed), pp. 1–2.

31. Ibid., p. 7.

32. This works two ways, however. We also need to have been receptive, attentive, and of service to our loved ones who are by definition more available to us and more supportive of us before we can assume the risk of these movements in more alien contexts. The situation is dialectical. The movements made in one context increase our resources for making them in the others.

33. Further discussion of this whole issue of contexts for the disciplines can be found in my "Christian Education and the Moral Life" (Ph.D. diss., Princeton Theological Seminary, 1978), pp. 203–20. Here these contexts are defined, their relationship to human development considered, and their bearing on one another more fully developed.

34. Edward Farley, in his *Ecclesial Man* (Philadelphia: Fortress Press, 1975), discusses "the transformed status of the stranger" in relation to the church. He puts the matter this way: "Insofar as the power of self-securing is broken and modified by freedom from the other and for the other, this power defines the very being of the participant of ecclesia. Thus, while the matrix of that power is ecclesia and its intersubjective structure, that toward which that power can be directed has no bounds. The new freedom is freedom for the other as such, not simply the other in ecclesia. The new obligation is for the other as such, not simply the ecclesial other" (pp. 169–70). Farley goes on to point out that while being for others as such includes a desire for mutuality, it does not place conditions on that mutuality. The church does not require that others become just like them in order for this mutuality to take place. "In ecclesia the stranger is . . . not . . . one who, to be redeemed, must abandon his own home-world but [is] a potential participant in ecclesia simply because of his disrupted humanity. . . . Since interest, delight, and compassion for the other are marks of freedom for the other, the stranger's status is that of fellow-sufferer and potential participant in redemptive existence. . . . [E]cclesia adapts its social and institutional form to the home-world of the stranger and not vice versa" (p. 170).

Chapter Five

1. This is, of course, quite a different perspective from the one that would argue that morality is an autonomous realm of human experience having universal features that define it, and that can be learned apart from any particular human community. From this perspective, which Kohlberg exemplifies, the moral life can be learned in any community. And no matter what community it is learned in, its basic features will be the same.

I do not disagree with the idea that the moral life can be learned in a variety of different communities. It can. The Christian community is not the only moral community, nor the only one that can help people to grow morally. What I do disagree with is the claim that there will not be fundamental differences between people who grow up morally in the various communities. Different communities have quite different understandings of what it means to be moral, what a morally exemplary person is like, what kinds of experiences are necessary for moral growth, and what convictions are fundamental to moral maturity. Even though there are many moral understandings that the various communities hold in common, it is not possible to say that they are all basically the same without ignoring much of what is most important within them. What Christians, and other communities, must do when they carry out moral education is to teach what the moral life means from *their* perspective, even while they recognize that this is not everyone's perspective.

What I have said here is an admission of relativism. Relativism is the great enemy of universalistic, juridical ethics. Universalism in ethics is not satisfied with a variety of moral points of view. It wishes to know what *the* moral point of view is, and is willing to go to great lengths to determine what it is. In the process, however, universalistic ethics often reduces differences to inessentials and thereby distorts its descriptions of how different communities actually understand the moral life. In addition, what often turns out to be essential to *the* moral point of view is just what is essential to its own moral point of view.

I have found H. Richard Niebuhr to be helpful in dealing with this problem of relativism. He admits that Christian theology is relativistic in the sense that its point of view is historically conditioned by its social setting and by the particular experiences the community has had (i.e., experiences of revelation) that other communities have not had. But he goes on to say that this "does not imply subjectivism and scepticism. It is not evident that the man who is forced to confess that his view of things is conditioned by the standpoint he occupies must doubt the reality of what he sees. It is not apparent that one who knows that his concepts are not universal must also doubt that they are concepts of the universal, or that one who understands how all his experience is historically mediated must believe that nothing is mediated through history" (*Meaning of Revelation* [New York: The Macmillan Co., 1960], p. 13).

Christians believe that what they see is true, and want to communicate that truth to others and invite them into this perspective to have a look for themselves. This belief does not, however, call for a defensive or aggressive attitude toward others who see things differently. The proper attitude is one of attention to what the other sees in order to learn from the other, and relaxed invitation to the other to come learn from this perspective.

2. The following quotations are taken from Bertram deH. Atwood, "Seeing the Invisible" (Unpublished sermon preached at the Grosse Pointe Memorial Church, Grosse Pointe, Michigan, July 30, 1967; mimeographed).

3. See C. Ellis Nelson, *Where Faith Begins* (Richmond: John Knox Press, 1967); John H. Westerhoff, III, *Values for Tomorrow's Children* (Philadelphia: Pilgrim Press, 1970), and idem, *Will Our Children Have Faith?* (New York: Seabury Press, 1976).

4. Martin Buber, *Between Man and Man,* trans. R. G. Smith (New York: The Macmillan Co., 1965), p. 106.

5. Ibid., p. 98.

6. No one is capable of such receptivity, attention, and service in all circumstances with all persons. I am only arguing that the disciplines of repentance, prayer, and service are learned, when they are learned, in the context of such relationships. Most of our attempts at teaching the disciplines of the moral life undoubtedly fail. Moral education is incredibly difficult. But when it does succeed, it is usually because such mutuality has to some degree been achieved.

7. Buber, *Between Man and Man,* p. 89.

8. Iris Murdoch, *The Sovereignty of Good* (New York: Schocken Books, 1970), p. 32.

9. John S. Stewart, "Problems and Contradictions of Values Clarification," in *Moral Education . . . It Comes with the Territory,* eds. D. Purpel and K. Ryan (Berkeley: McCutchan Publishing Corp., 1976), pp. 141–42.

10. A significant six-year liturgical experiment was undertaken in Brussels in which worship provided a profound medium of interpretation of moral conflicts. See Herman Lombaerts, "Reciprocal Relationships between Moral Commitment and Faith Profession in Worship," in *Toward Moral and Religious Maturity: The First International Conference on Moral and Religious Development,* Christiane Brusselmans, convenor (Morristown, N.J.: Silver Burdett Co., 1980), pp. 251–76, for a description and analysis of this experiment.

11. C. Daniel Batson, "Creativity and Religious Development: Toward a Structural-Functional Psychology of Religion" (Th.D. diss. Princeton Theological Seminary, 1971), p. 315.

12. Frederick Buechner, *Telling the Truth: The Gospel as Tragedy, Comedy, and Fairy Tale* (New York: Harper & Row, 1977), p. 81.

13. Ibid., p. 90.

14. Ibid., p. 78.

15. See my editorial, "My Teacher, We Made Bread...," *Christian Century* 97 (October 1, 1980): 901–02, for a more extended exegesis of my son's comment.

16. Philip P. Haillie, "Comments in a Symposium on Morality," *The American Scholar* 34 (1965): 365.

17. Donald Vandenburg, "Life-phases and Values," *Educational Forum* 32 (1968): 296.

18. Ibid.

19. Murdoch, *Sovereignty of Good,* p. 67.

20. Murdoch, "Vision and Choice in Morality," in Ramsey, *Christian Ethics and Contemporary Philosophy,* p. 208.